VOLUME 1
Elementary - Intermediate

ENCYCLOPEDIA OF CLASSICAL PIANO MUSIC

Compiled and Edited by
Robert Schultz & Tina Faigen

T0007103

PIANO SOLOS
BY THE
GREAT COMPOSERS

Production: Frank and Gail Hackinson
Production Coordinator: Derek Richard
Editors: Robert Schultz and Dr. Tina Faigen
Cover: Terpstra Design, San Francisco
Engraving: Tempo Music Press, Inc.
Printer: Tempo Music Press, Inc.

ISBN 1-56939-361-3

ROBERT SCHULTZ, composer, arranger, and editor, has achieved international fame during his career in the music publishing industry. The Schultz Piano Library, established in 1980, has included more than 500 publications of classical works, popular arrangements, and Schultz's original compositions in editions for pianists of every level from the beginner through the concert artist. In addition to his extensive library of published piano works, Schultz's output includes original orchestral works, chamber music, works for solo instruments, and vocal music. He currently devotes his full time to composing and arranging, writing from his studio in Miami, Florida.

Schultz has presented his published editions at workshops, clinics, and convention showcases throughout the United States and Canada. He is frequently engaged as an adjudicator for piano competitions and composition contests. Schultz is a long-standing member of ASCAP, has served as president of the Miami Music Teachers Association, and is an active member of numerous other professional music organizations. Schultz's original piano compositions and transcriptions are featured on the compact disc recordings *Visions of Dunbar* and *Tina Faigen Plays Piano Transcriptions*, released on the ACA Digital label and available worldwide. His published original works for concert artists are noted in Maurice Hinson's *Guide to the Pianist's Repertoire, Third Edition*. Outstanding reviews in *The American Music Teacher, Clavier, Piano Quarterly*, and numerous other music periodicals reflect the enthusiasm with which his piano works have been received. In-depth information about Robert Schultz and The Schultz Piano Library is available at the Web site www.schultzmusic.com.

DR. TINA FAIGEN is a concert pianist, recording artist, teacher, and editor. In addition to performing as a recitalist and chamber musician, she has been engaged as guest soloist with orchestras in the United States and Europe, including the Pittsburgh Symphony at the age of 13. Music critics have described her as "commanding a rich palette of pianistic colors and fingers of awesome dexterity," and as having "a compelling combination of solid technique and distinctive interpretation, full of color and nuance, with her virtuosity the servant of the music. A stunning performer who plays with assurance, fluidity and power."

Faigen has maintained an active private teaching studio since she was 14 and continues to guide students of all ages and levels of ability. In 1992, she carried her expertise into the field of music editing, serving as the principal music editor for The Schultz Piano Library, which includes editions of standard classical repertoire and Schultz's original works, arrangements, and piano transcriptions. Faigen's compact disc recordings of Schultz's works—*Visions of Dunbar* and *Tina Faigen Plays Piano Transcriptions*—have received rave reviews. "Faigen plays Schultz's works superlatively, effortlessly clarifying their rippling complexities and performing with supple dexterity, a clear, resonant tone and sensitive touch."

Faigen holds three degrees in piano performance. She earned her Doctor of Musical Arts and Master of Music degrees from the University of Miami, and her Bachelor of Music degree from Oberlin College Conservatory of Music.

Preface

Encyclopedia of Classical Piano Music, Volume 1 is created to serve as a permanent edition in the music library of every pianist—students, teachers, professionals, and amateurs. The collection includes 85 piano solos, 75 of which are standard classical piano works in their original form, and 10 of which are piano arrangements of classical masterpieces from the orchestral, vocal, and chamber music literature of the great composers. Thirty-one famous composers are represented, whose works span more than 400 years of music history.

The music selected for this volume ranges in difficulty from the elementary level to the intermediate level, and includes works traditionally used to introduce student pianists to the literature of the great composers. The contents are divided into five main sections. Each of the first four sections is devoted to a specific period in music history and contains only works that were originally composed for the piano. These pieces are grouped by composers and are presented in their complete, original form. The fifth section includes piano arrangements of orchestral and other well-known, non-piano works, such as Pachelbel's *Canon In D,* Elgar's *Pomp and Circumstance,* and *The Wedding March* from Mendelssohn's *A Midsummer Night's Dream.*

Each piece is precisely edited with utmost respect for the intention of the composer and the performance practice of the period. While some phrasing, dynamics, articulations, pedaling, and necessary fingering has been added to guide the performer, great care has been taken to avoid overediting. Ornaments are displayed in their traditional symbol format. The realization of baroque ornaments appears directly above the symbol to provide a clear indication of how the ornament is to be interpreted. Additional reference material appears in the back of the book. Included are a table of music symbols, a list of relevant tempo marks, a complete glossary of the music terms used herein, a title index, and the dates of the composers.

Contents

THE BAROQUE PERIOD

THE CLASSICAL PERIOD

THE ROMANTIC PERIOD

THE TWENTIETH CENTURY

ARRANGEMENTS OF ORCHESTRAL, VOCAL, & CHAMBER WORKS

THE
BAROQUE PERIOD

(1600 – 1750)

MINUET

from the Notebook for
Anna Magdalena Bach

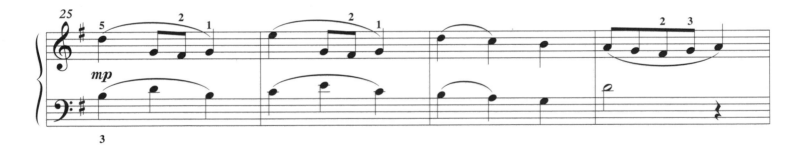

MINUET

from the Notebook for
Anna Magdalena Bach

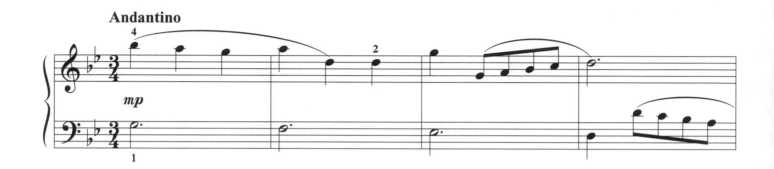

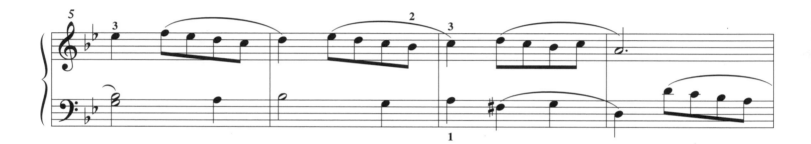

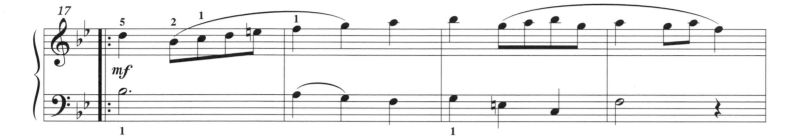

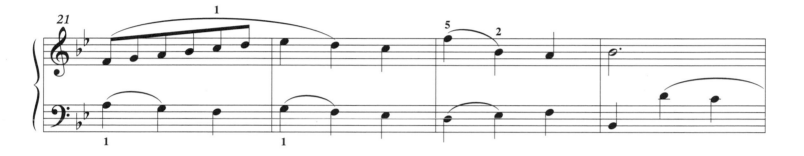

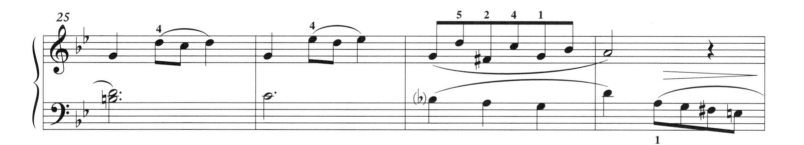

MINUET

from the Notebook for
Anna Magdalena Bach

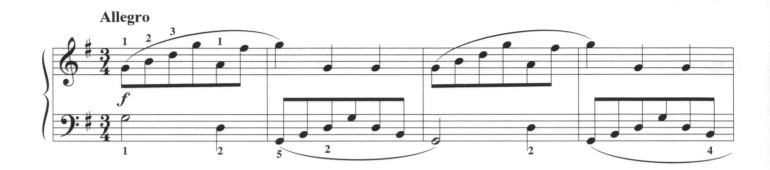

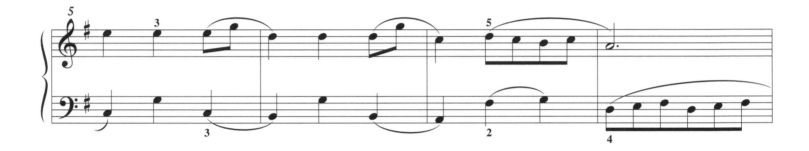

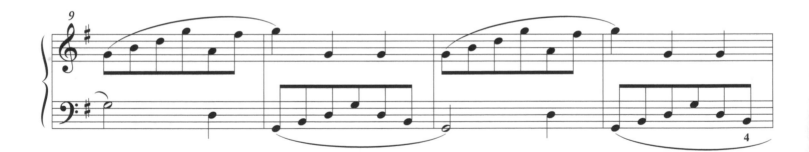

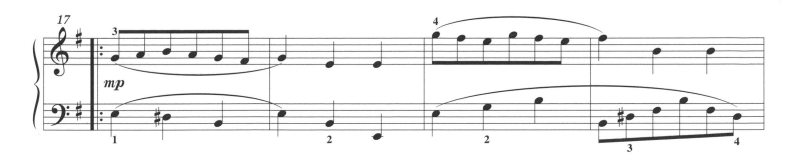

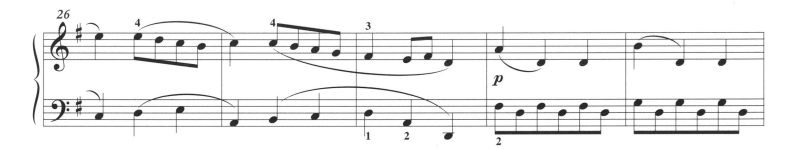

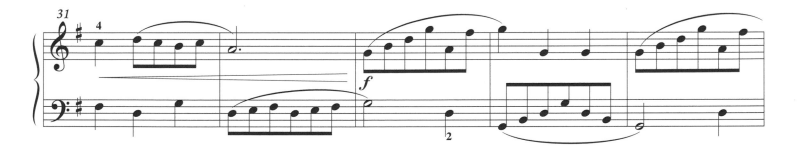

MINUET

from the Notebook for
Anna Magdalena Bach

Allegretto

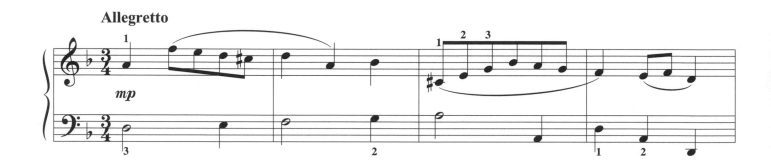

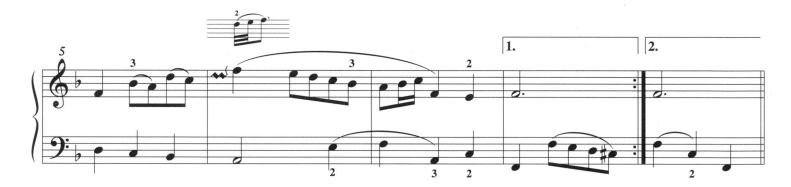

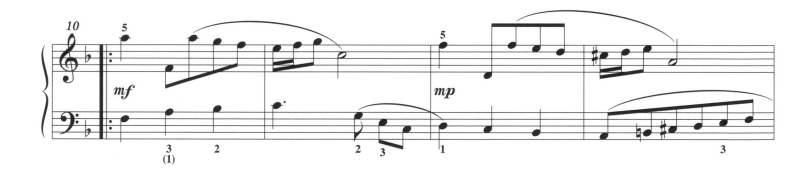

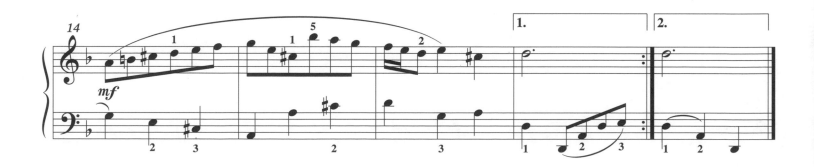

POLONAISE

from the Notebook for
Anna Magdalena Bach

Moderato

FF1392

MARCH

from the Notebook for
Anna Magdalena Bach

Allegro moderato

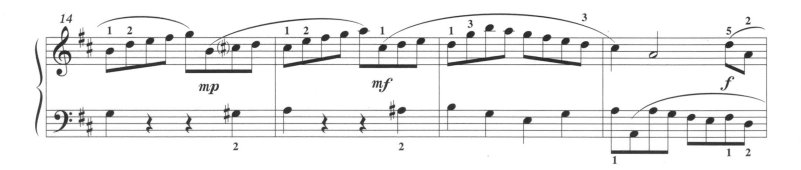

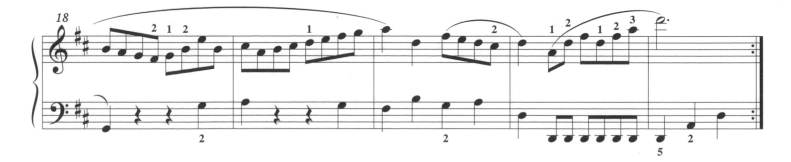

MARCH

from the Notebook for
Anna Magdalena Bach

SOLFEGGIETTO

CARL PHILIPP EMANUEL BACH

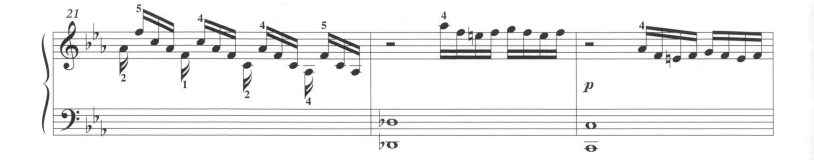

PRELUDE

(from *The Well-Tempered Clavier Book I*)

JOHANN SEBASTIAN BACH
BWV 846

PRELUDE

(No. 1 from *5 Little Preludes*)

JOHANN SEBASTIAN BACH
BWV 939

Moderato

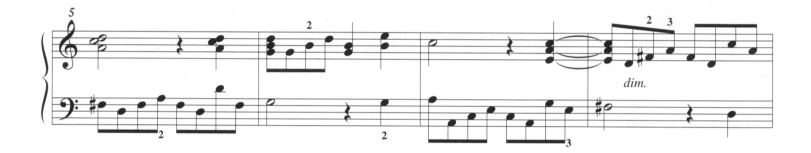

PRELUDE

(No. 6 from *6 Little Preludes*)

JOHANN SEBASTIAN BACH
BWV 999

Con moto

26

FF1392

PRELUDE

(No. 2 from *W. F. Bach Notebook*)

JOHANN SEBASTIAN BACH
BWV 926

Moderato

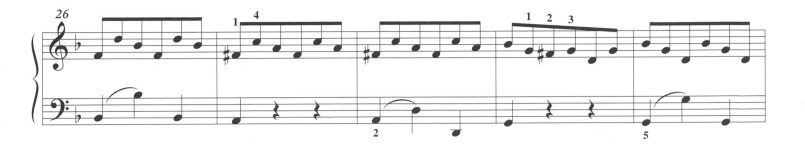

GAVOTTE

ARCANGELO CORELLI

Allegro moderato

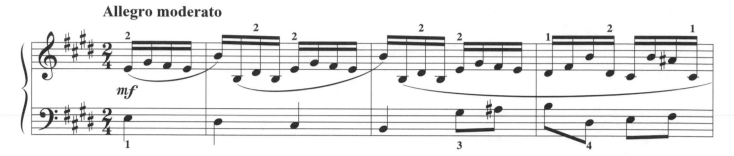

GAVOTTE

GEORGE FRIDERIC HANDEL

Allegro moderato

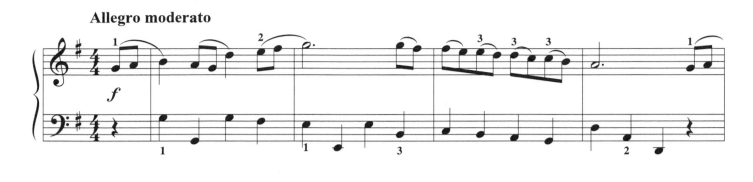

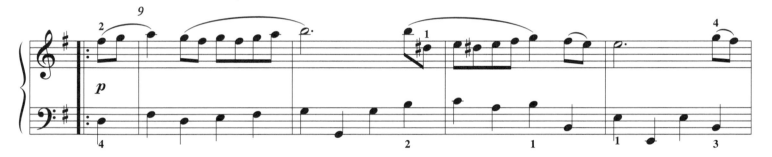

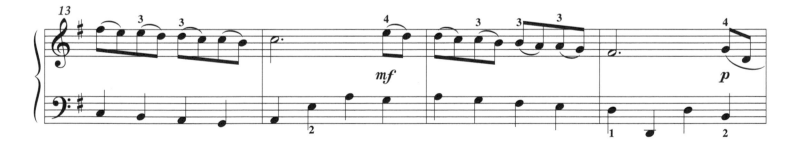

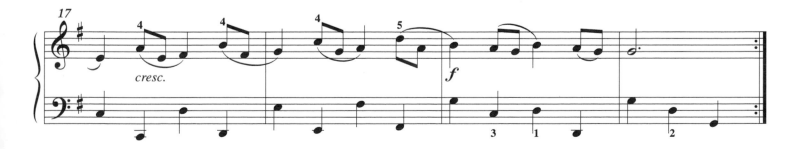

MINUET

GEORGE FRIDERIC HANDEL

Moderato

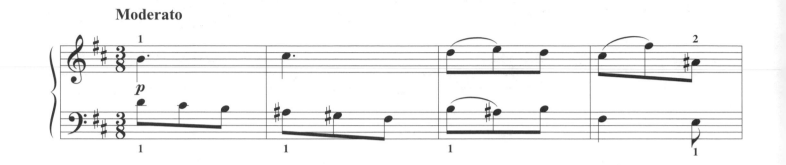

MINUET

GEORGE FRIDERIC HANDEL

Allegretto

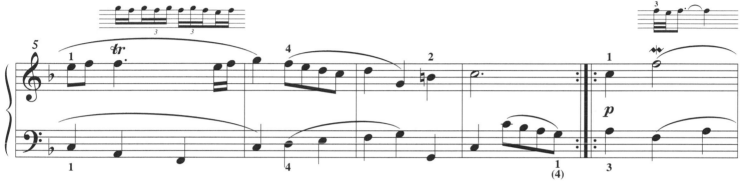

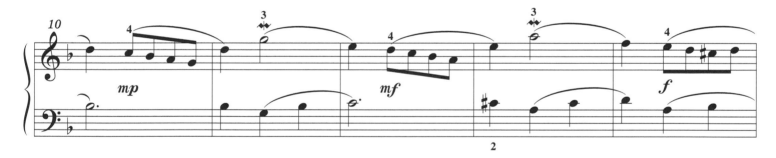

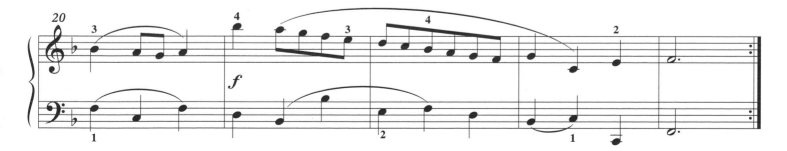

IMPERTINENCE

GEORGE FRIDERIC HANDEL

Allegretto

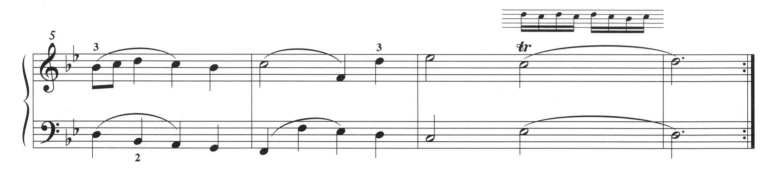

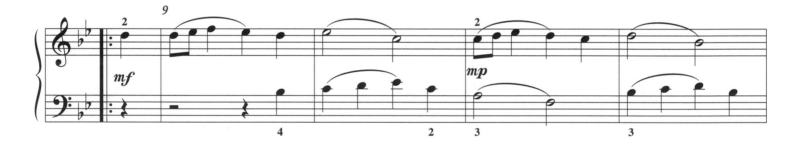

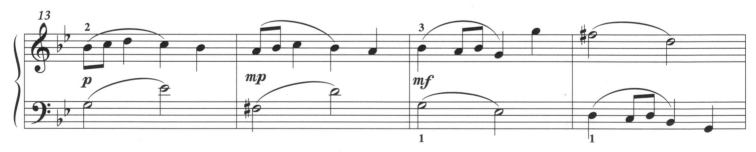

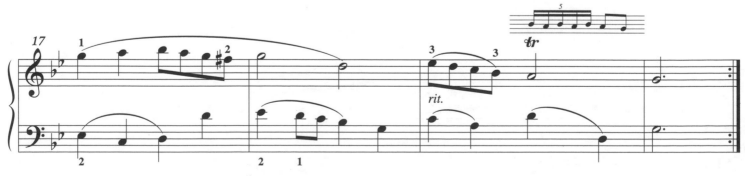

ARIA

DOMENICO SCARLATTI
K. 32

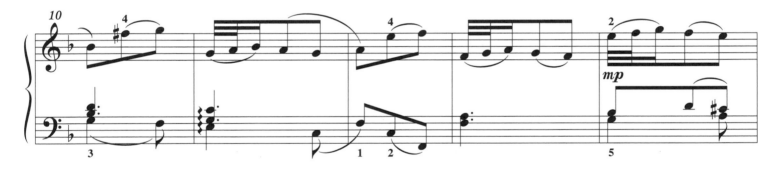

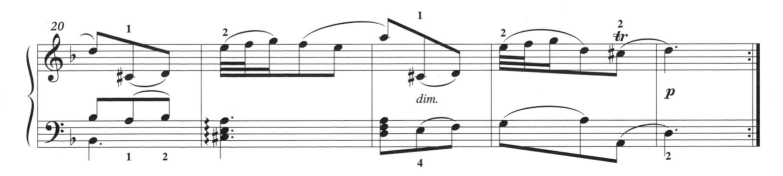

MINUET

DOMENICO SCARLATTI
K. 73b

Allegro moderato

SONATA

DOMENICO SCARLATTI
K. 89b

Grave

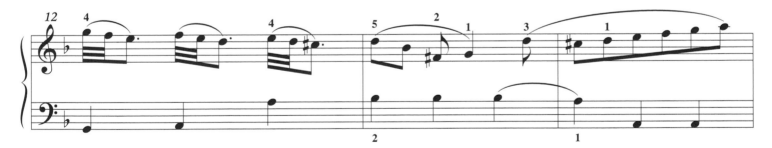

SONATA

DOMENICO SCARLATTI
K. 34

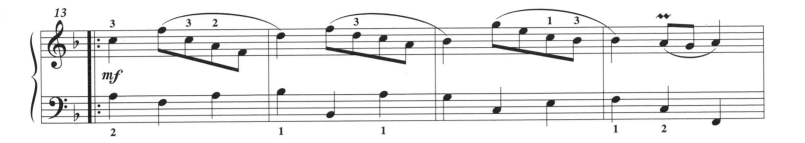

MINUET

GEORG PHILIPP TELEMANN

Allegretto

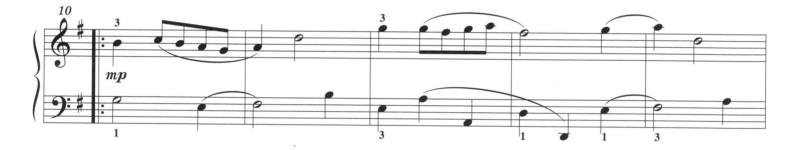

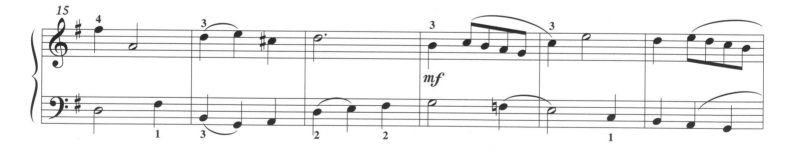

GIGUE

GEORG PHILIPP TELEMANN

Allegro

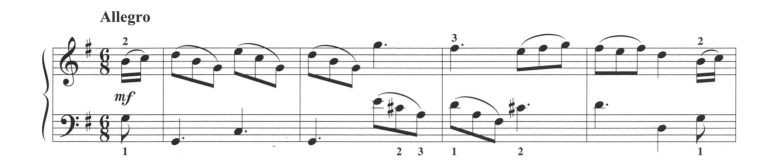

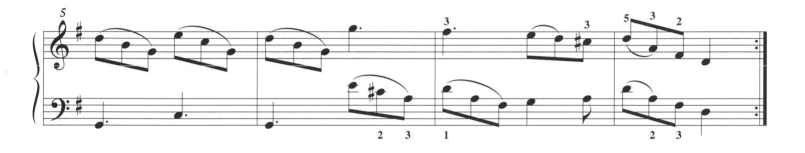

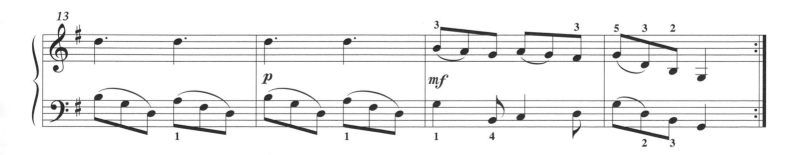

THE
CLASSICAL PERIOD
(1750 – 1820)

ÉCOSSAISE

LUDWIG VAN BEETHOVEN
K. WoO 23

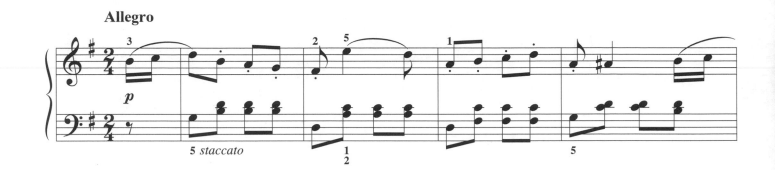

GERMAN DANCE

LUDWIG VAN BEETHOVEN

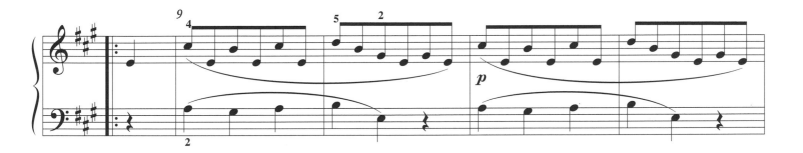

FÜR ELISE

LUDWIG VAN BEETHOVEN
K. WoO 59

Poco moto

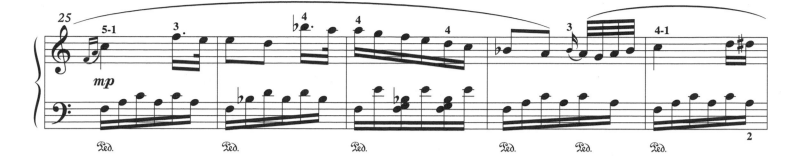

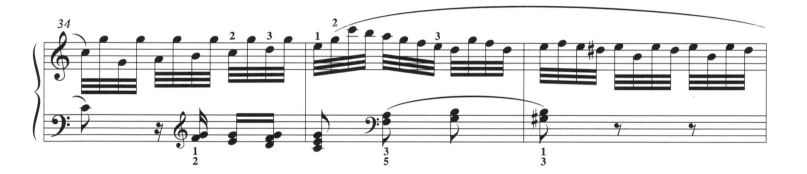

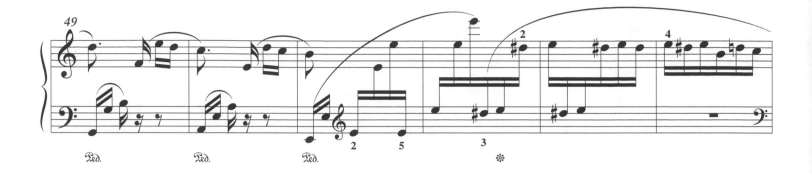

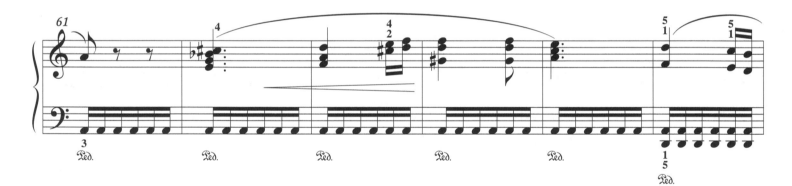

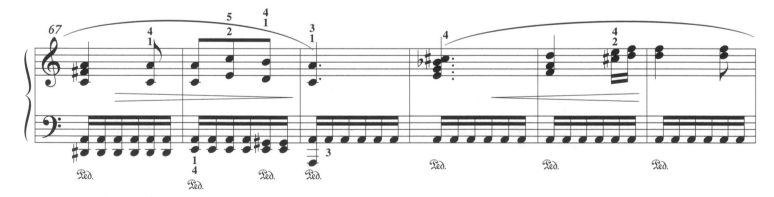

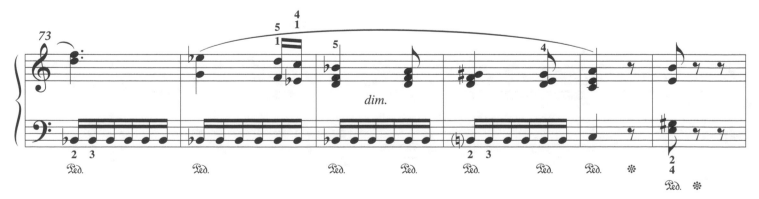

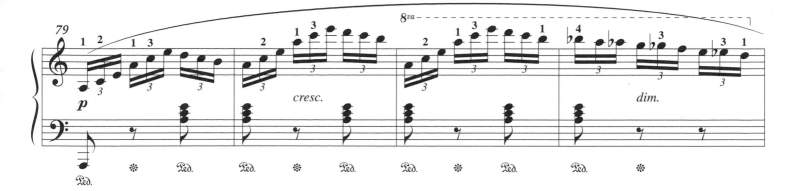

SONATINA

I

LUDWIG VAN BEETHOVEN

Moderato

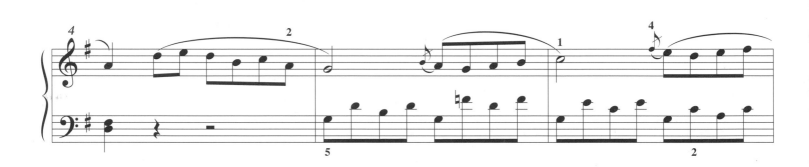

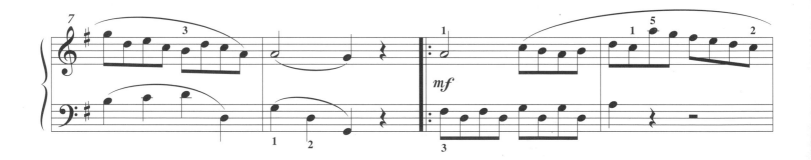

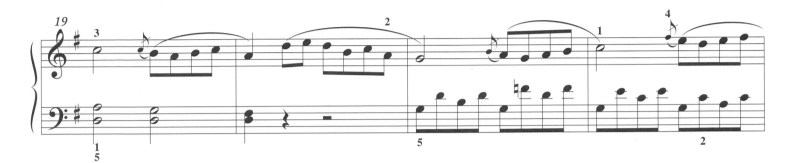

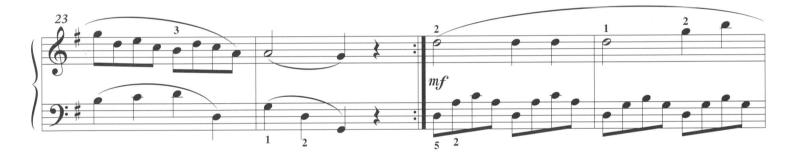

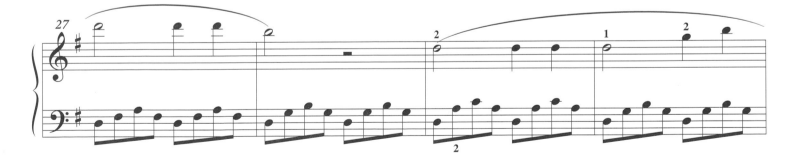

II

Romanze

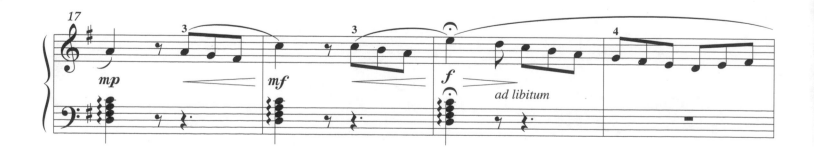

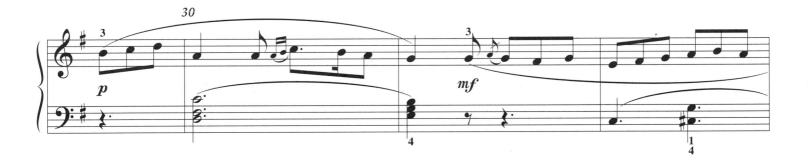

SONATINA
I

MUZIO CLEMENTI
Op. 36, No. 1

Allegro

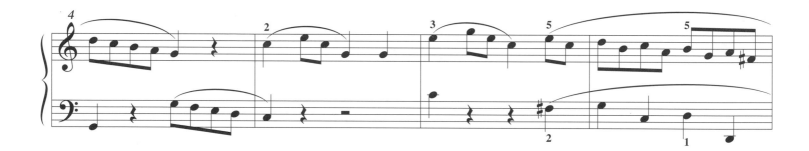

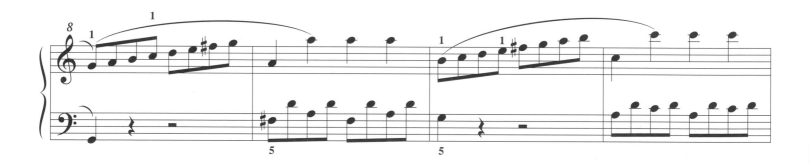

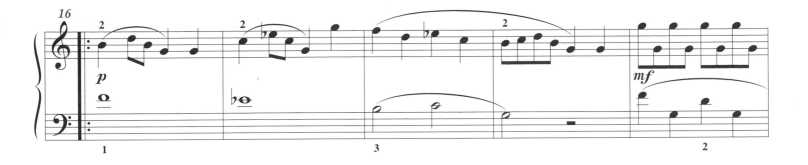

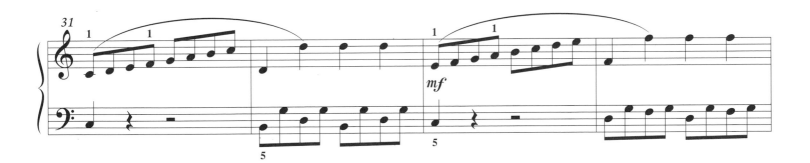

II

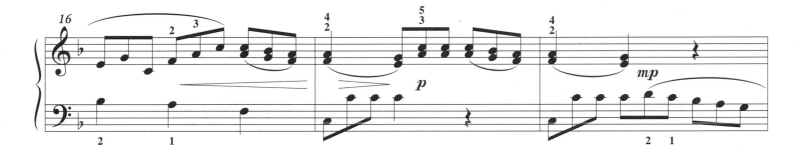

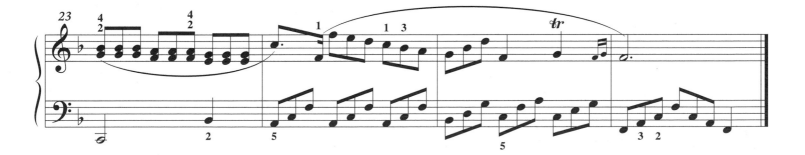

III

Vivace

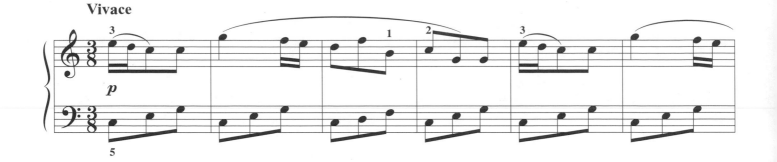

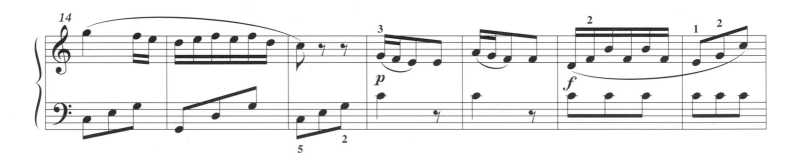

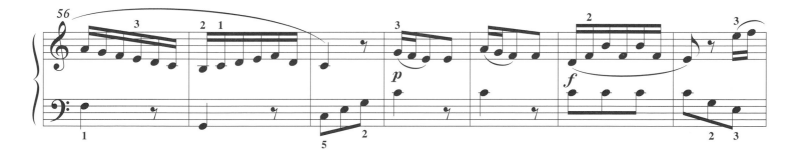

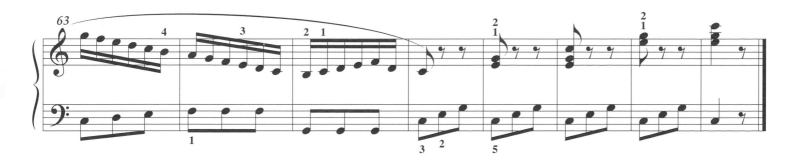

SONATINA
I

MUZIO CLEMENTI
Op. 36, No. 3

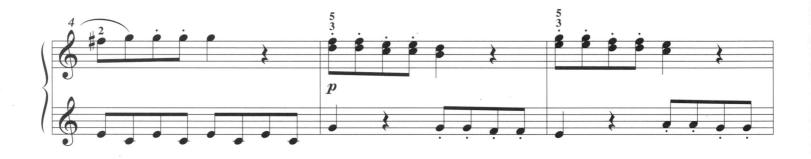

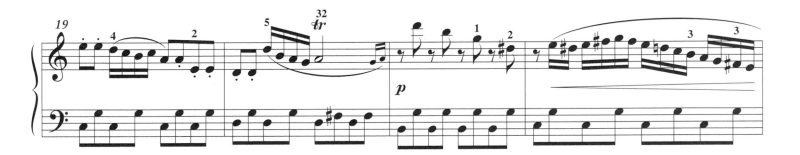

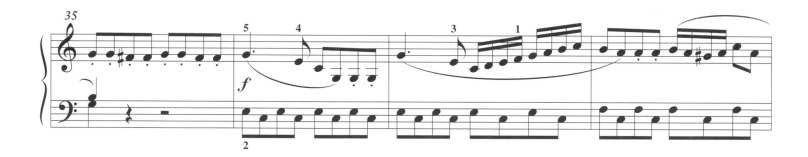

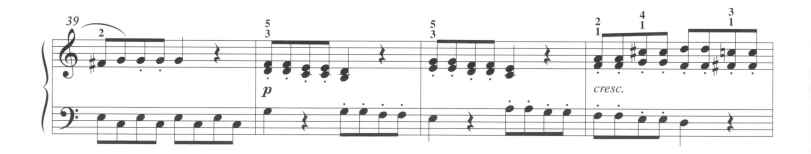

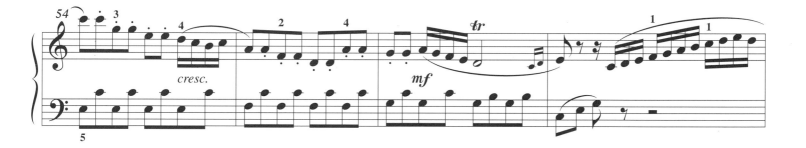

II

Un poco adagio

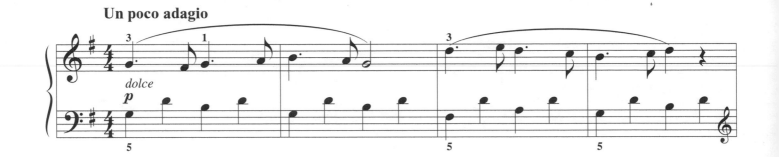

III

Allegro

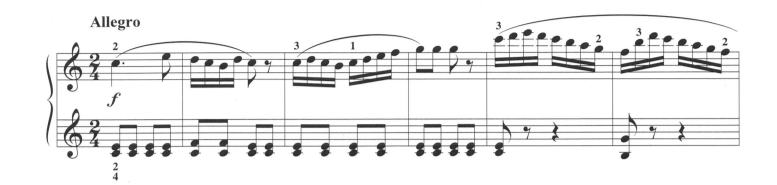

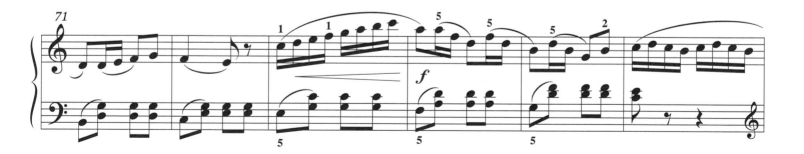

ALLEGRETTO

FRANZ JOSEPH HAYDN

Allegretto

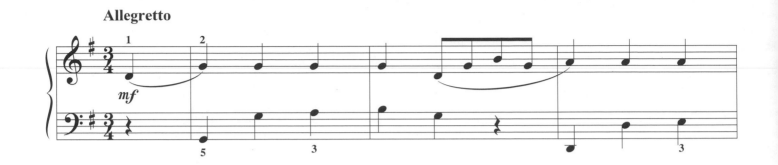

GERMAN DANCE

FRANZ JOSEPH HAYDN

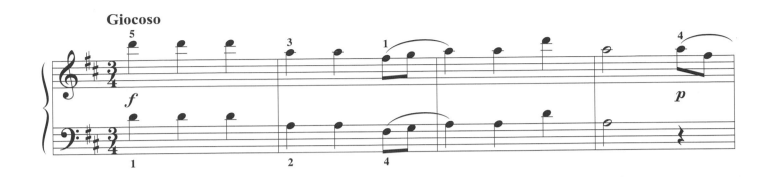

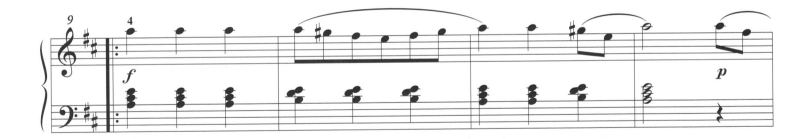

GERMAN DANCE

FRANZ JOSEPH HAYDN

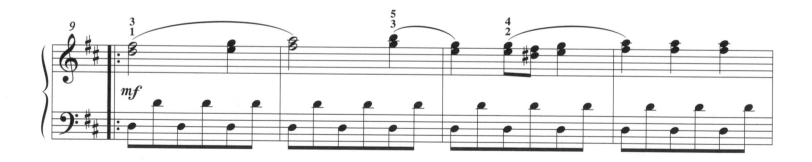

GERMAN DANCE

FRANZ JOSEPH HAYDN

Moderato

SONATINA

I

FRIEDRICH KUHLAU
Op. 20, No. 1

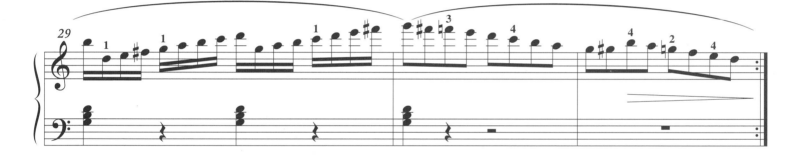

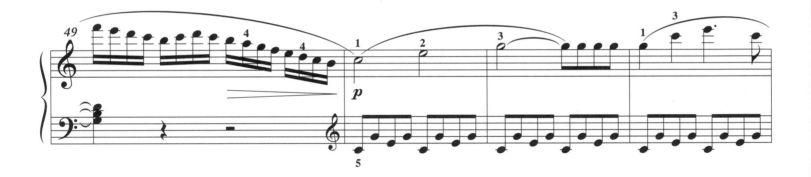

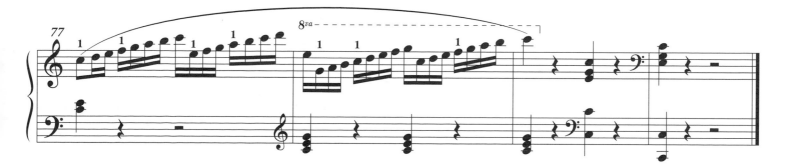

II

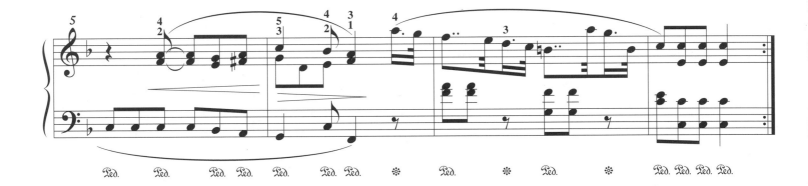

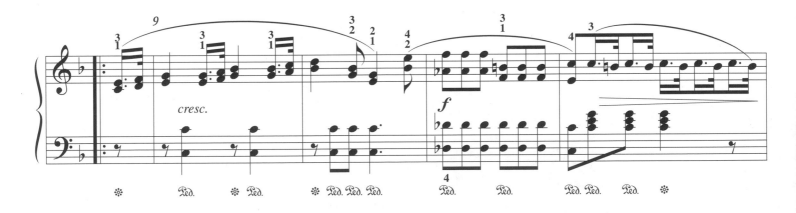

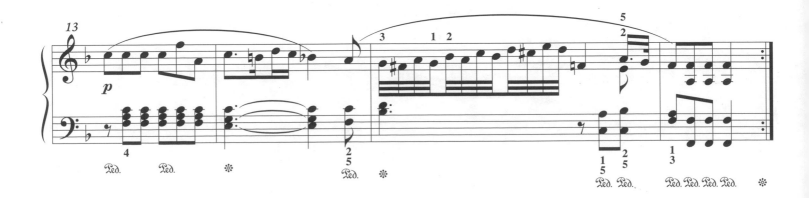

III

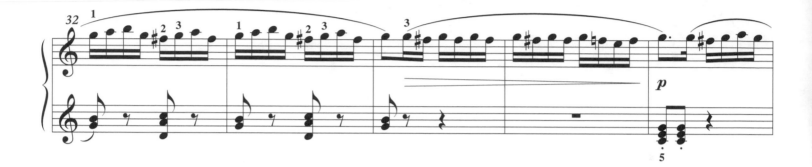

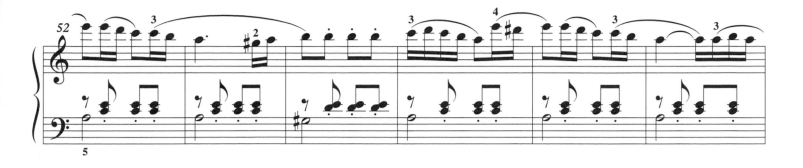

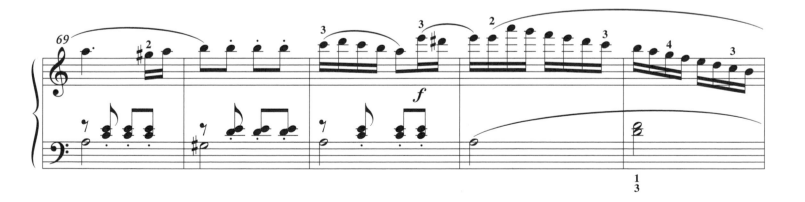

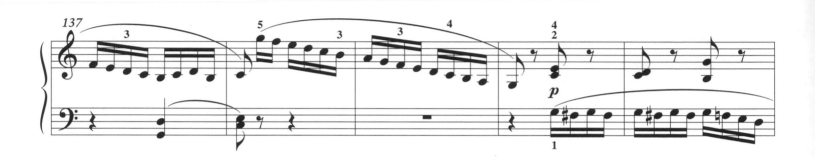

MINUET

(from *Nannerl's Notebook*)

LEOPOLD MOZART

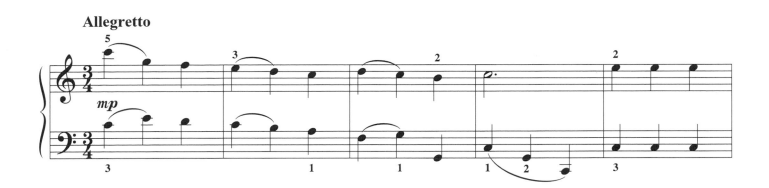

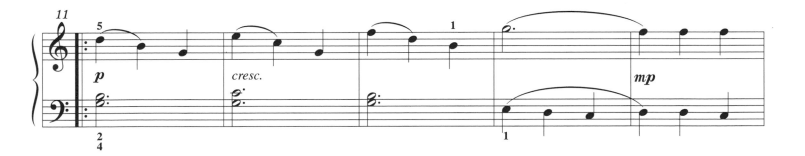

MINUET
(from *Nannerl's Notebook*)

LEOPOLD MOZART

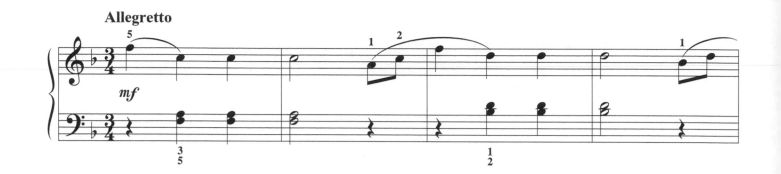

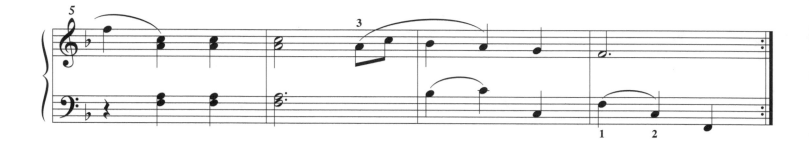

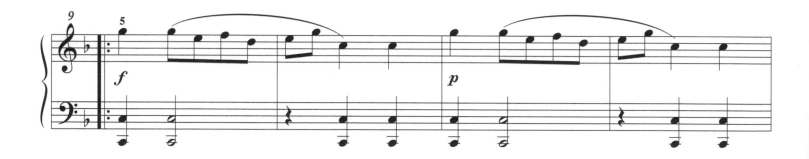

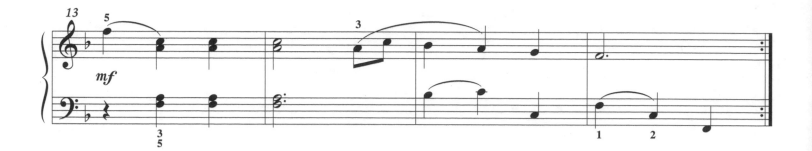

MINUET

(from *Nannerl's Notebook*)

LEOPOLD MOZART

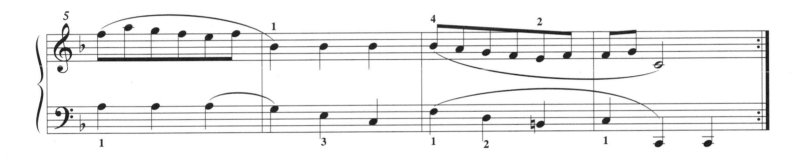

ALLEGRO

(from *Nannerl's Notebook*)

WOLFGANG AMADEUS MOZART
K. 3

MINUET

(from *Nannerl's Notebook*)

WOLFGANG AMADEUS MOZART
K. 3

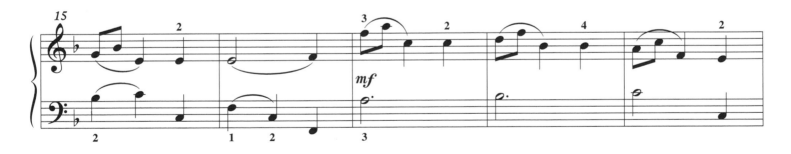

MINUET AND TRIO

(from *Nannerl's Notebook*)

WOLFGANG AMADEUS MOZART
K. 1

Allegretto

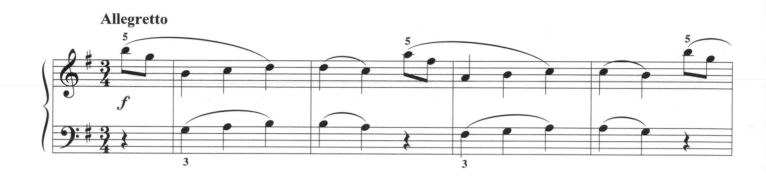

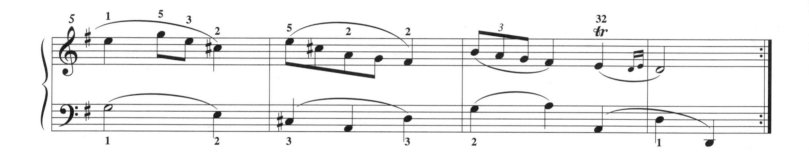

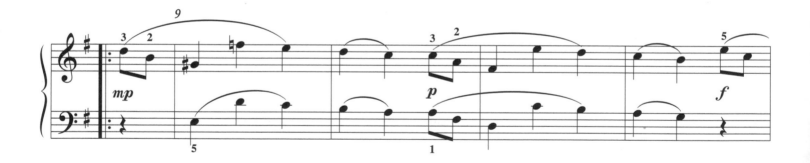

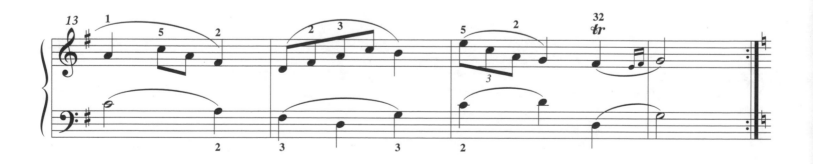

Trio

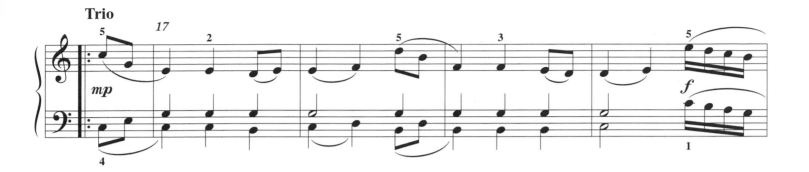

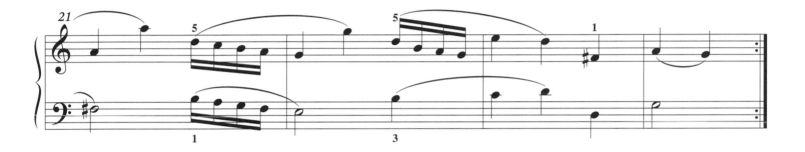

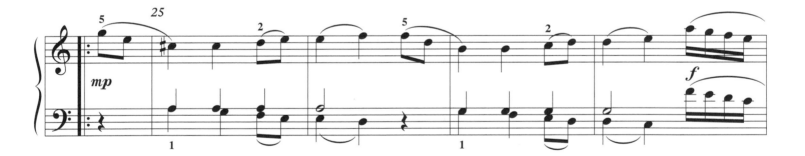

Minuet da Capo

MINUET

(from *Nannerl's Notebook*)

WOLFGANG AMADEUS MOZART
K. 5

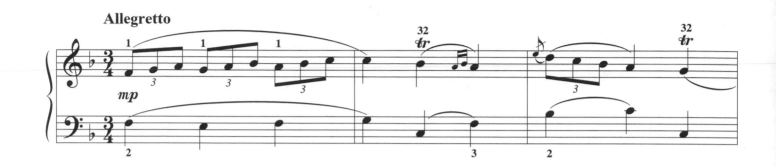

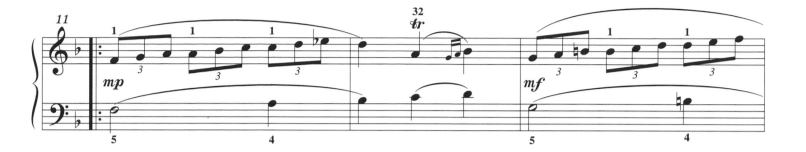

MINUET

(from *Nannerl's Notebook*)

WOLFGANG AMADEUS MOZART
K. 6

Allegretto

MINUET
(from *Nannerl's Notebook*)

WOLFGANG AMADEUS MOZART
K. 7

Moderato

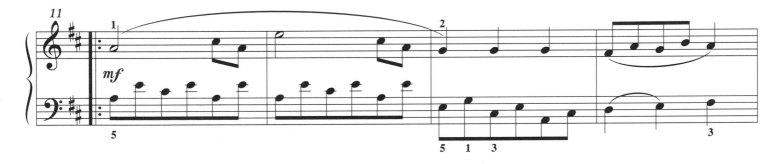

EVENING SONG

DANIEL GOTTLOB TÜRK

Andante

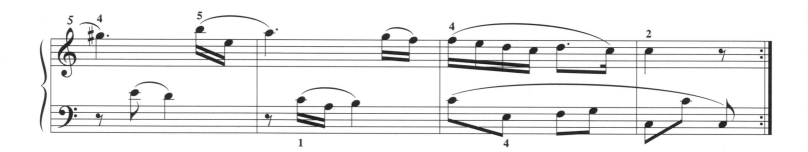

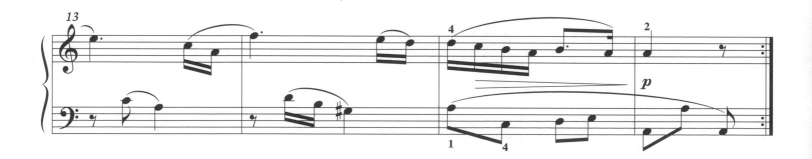

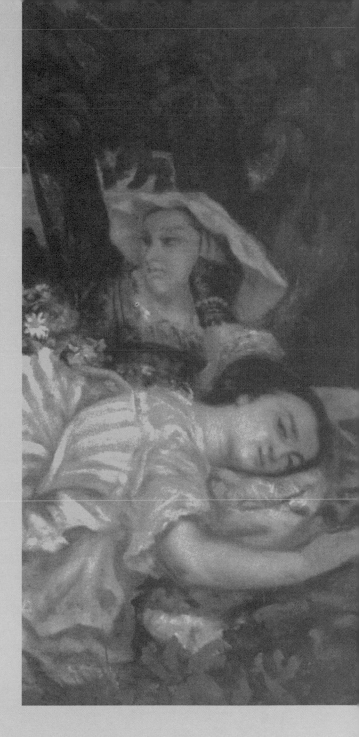

THE
ROMANTIC PERIOD

(1820 – 1900)

ARABESQUE

JOHANN FRIEDRICH BURGMÜLLER
Op. 100, No. 2

Allegro scherzando

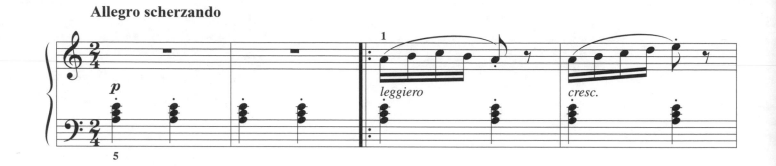

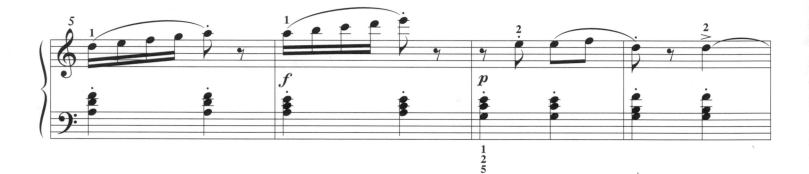

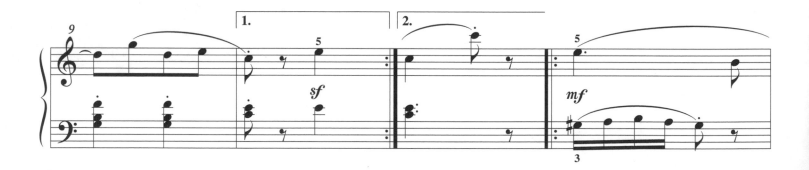

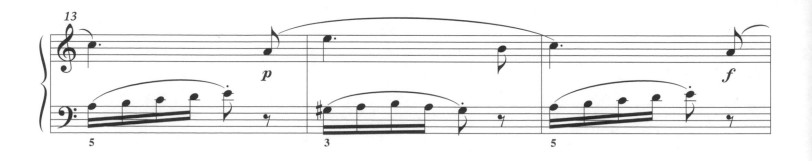

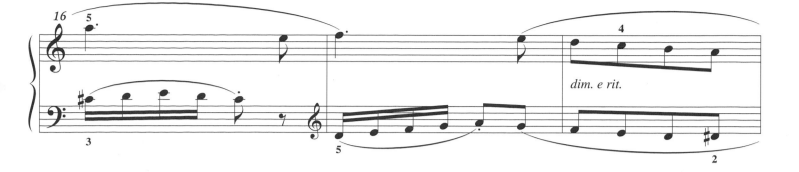

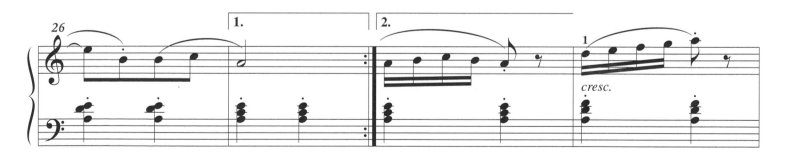

BALLADE

JOHANN FRIEDRICH BURGMÜLLER
Op. 100, No. 15

Allegro con brio

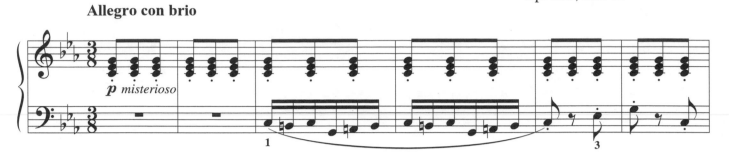

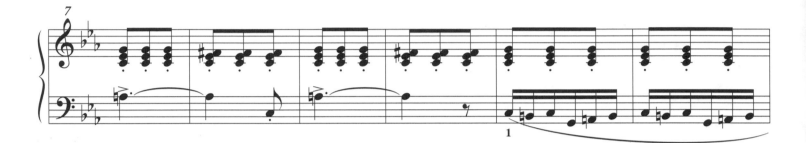

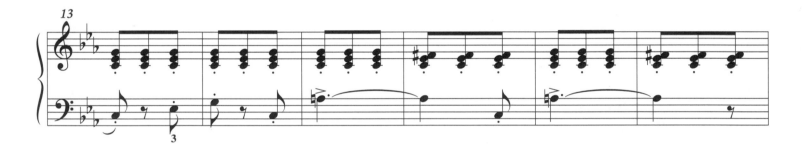

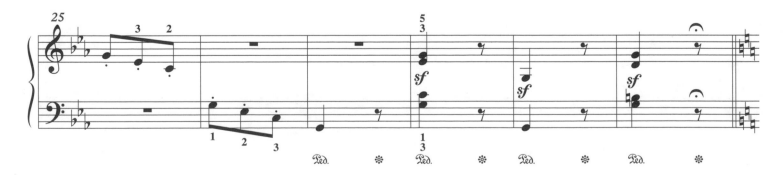

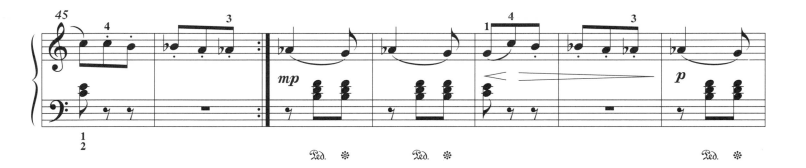

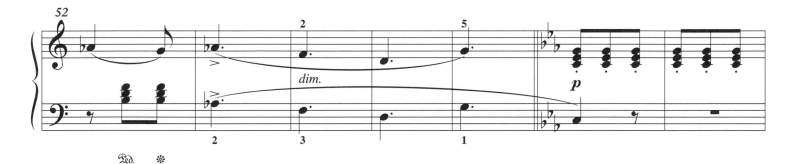

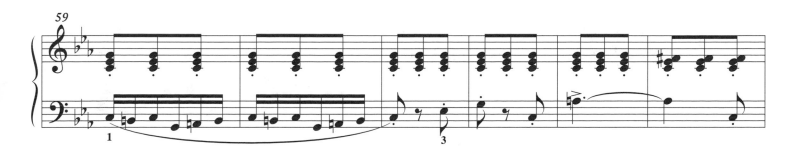

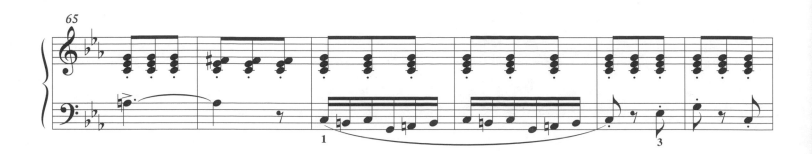

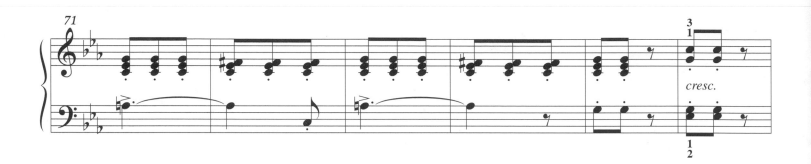

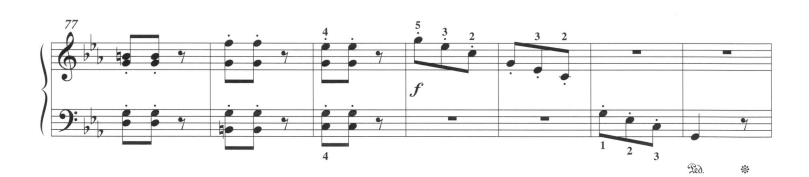

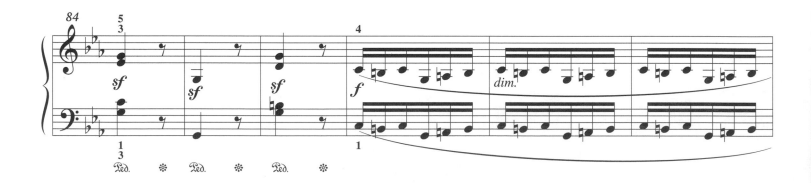

FF1392

WALTZ
(Posthumous)

FRÉDÉRIC CHOPIN

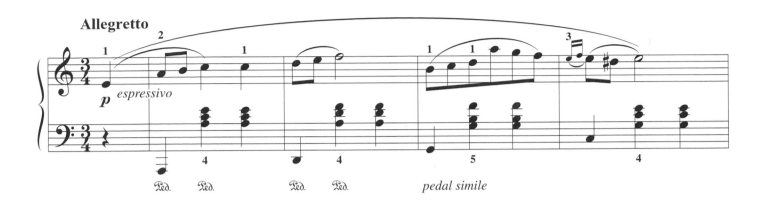

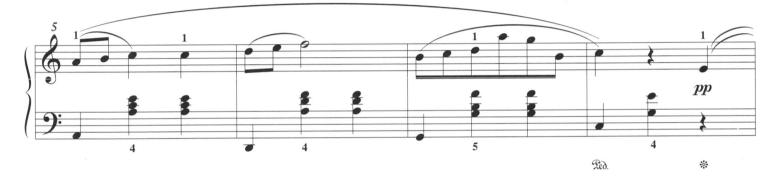

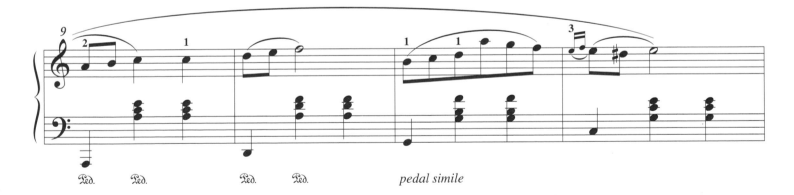

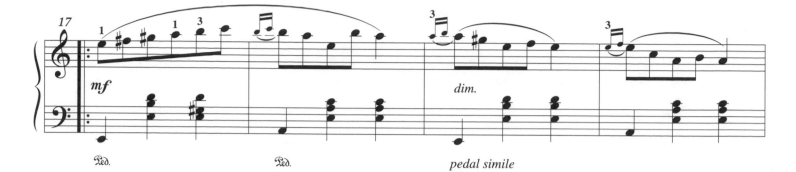

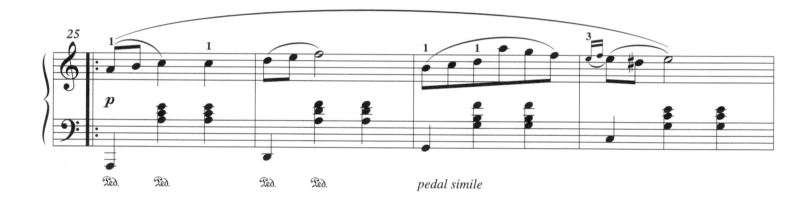

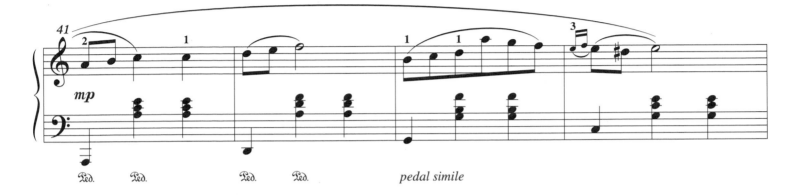

FF1392

MAZURKA

FRÉDÉRIC CHOPIN
Op. 67, No. 2

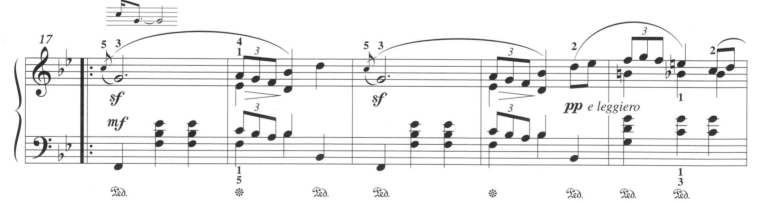

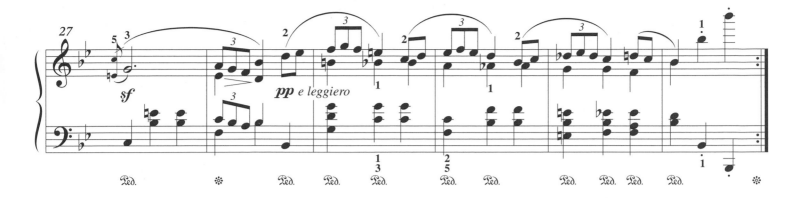

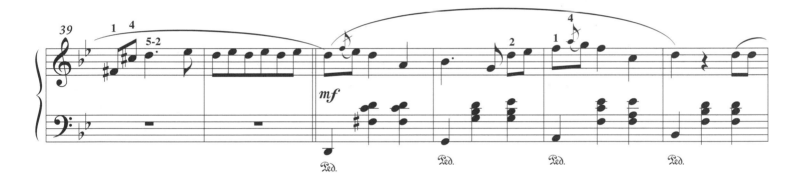

PRELUDE

FRÉDÉRIC CHOPIN
Op. 28, No. 4

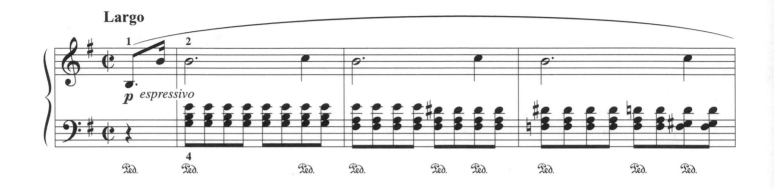

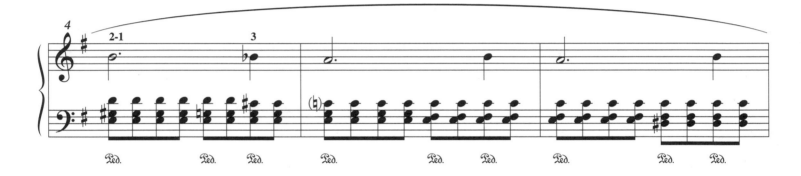

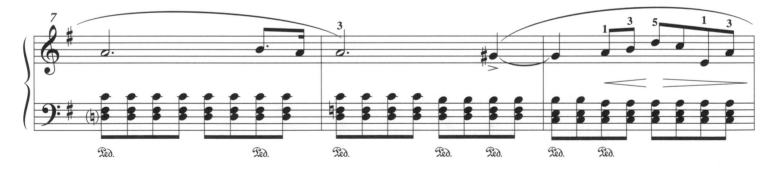

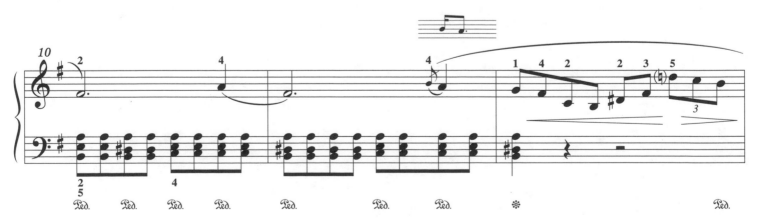

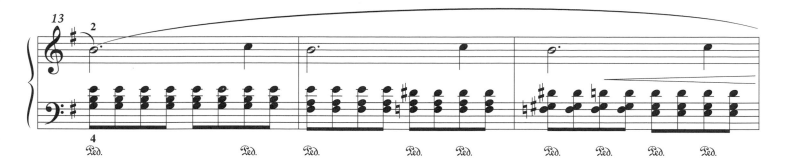

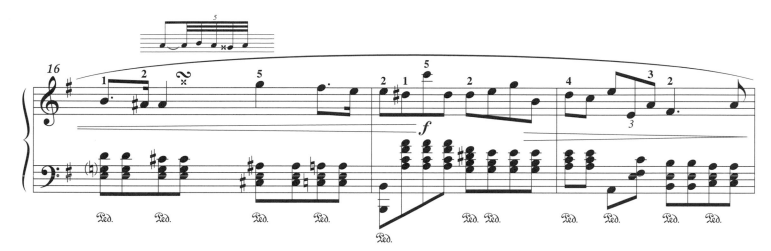

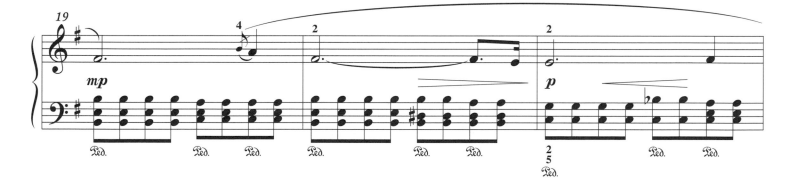

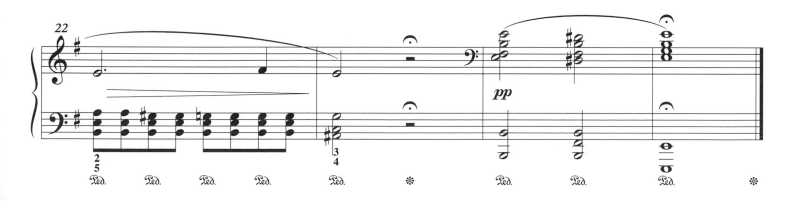

PRELUDE

FRÉDÉRIC CHOPIN
Op. 28, No. 6

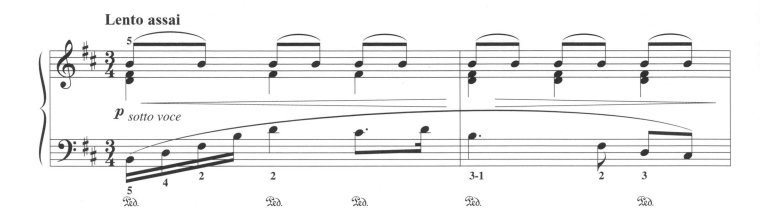

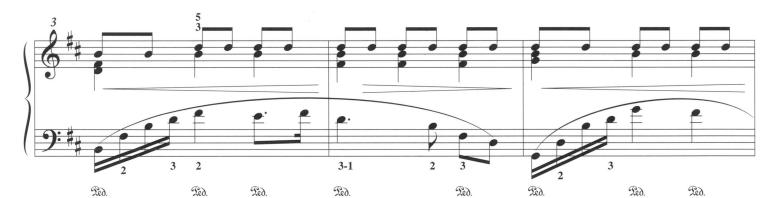

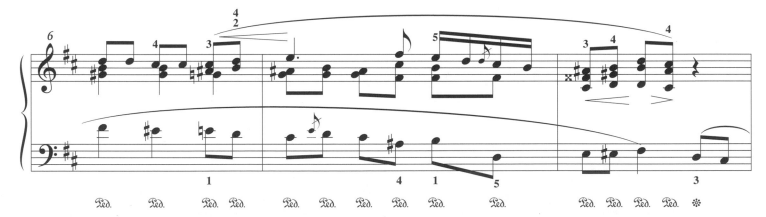

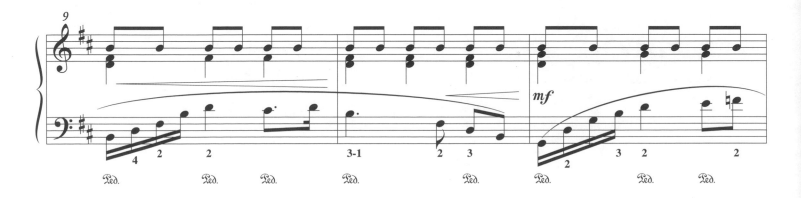

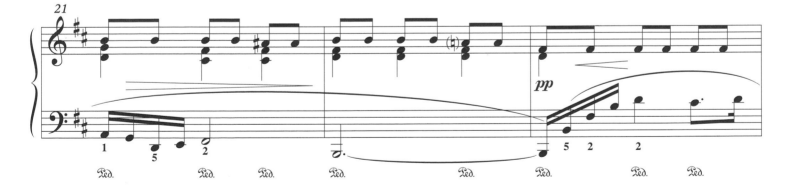

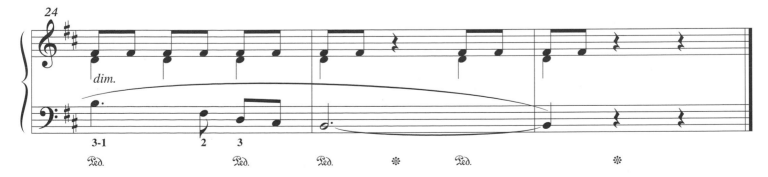

PRELUDE

FRÉDÉRIC CHOPIN
Op. 28, No. 7

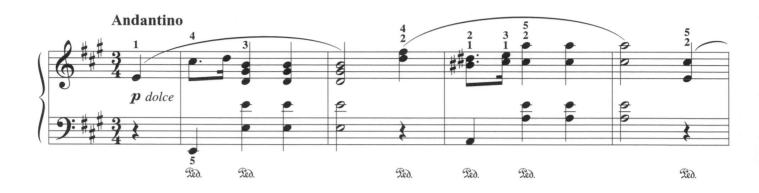

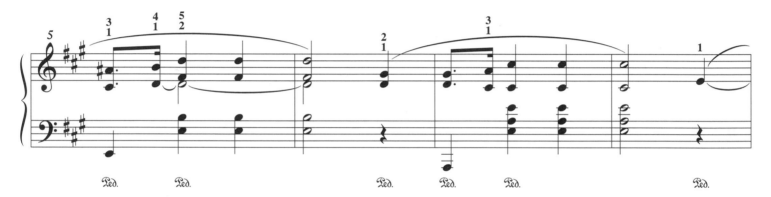

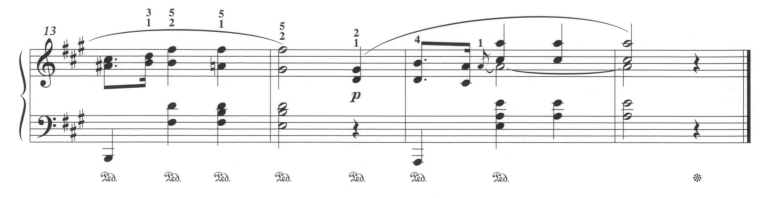

PRELUDE

FRÉDÉRIC CHOPIN
Op. 28, No. 20

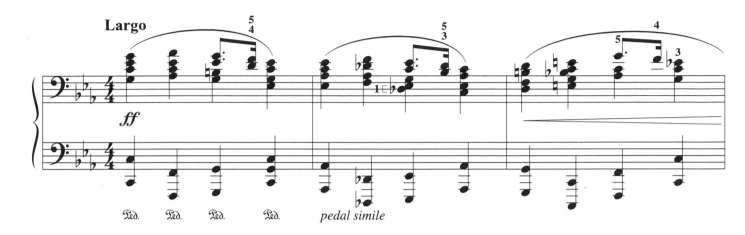

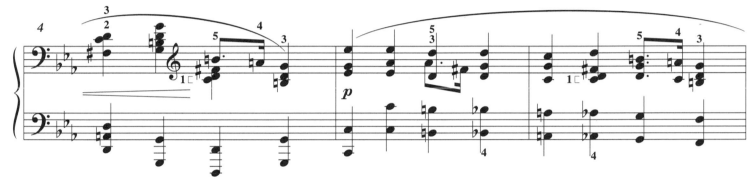

TO A WILD ROSE

EDWARD MacDOWELL
Op. 51, No. 1

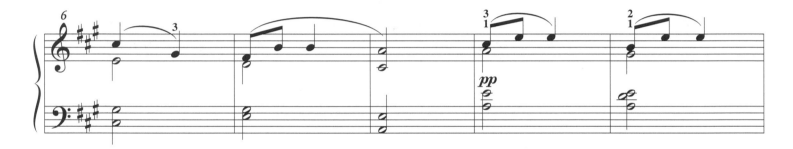

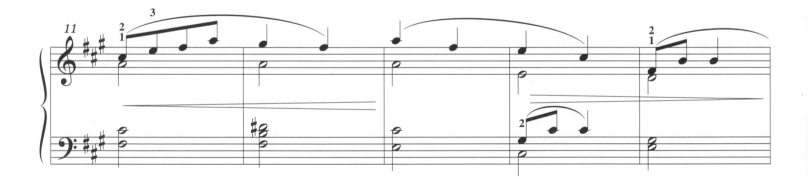

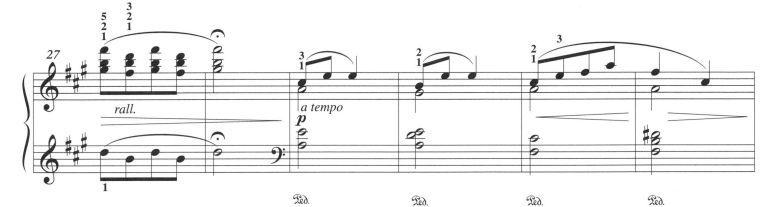

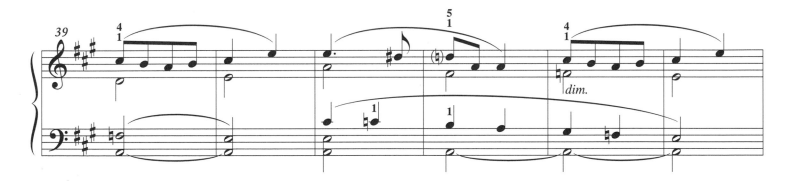

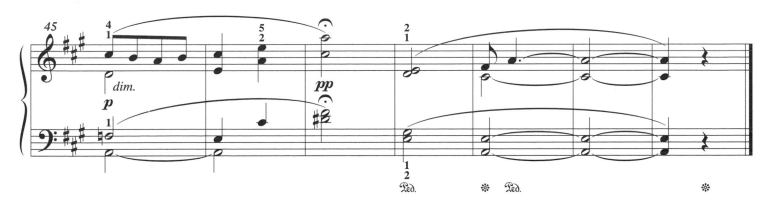

WALTZ

FRANZ SCHUBERT

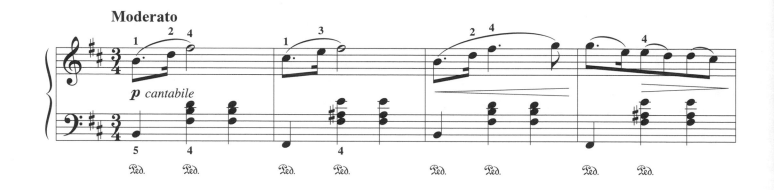

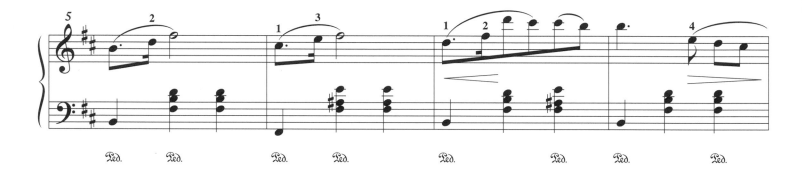

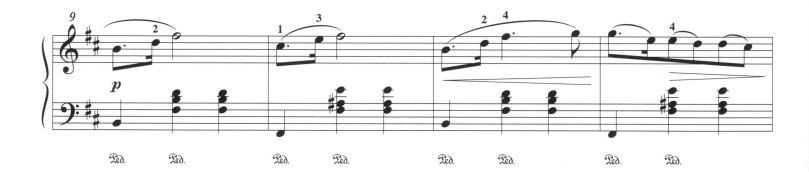

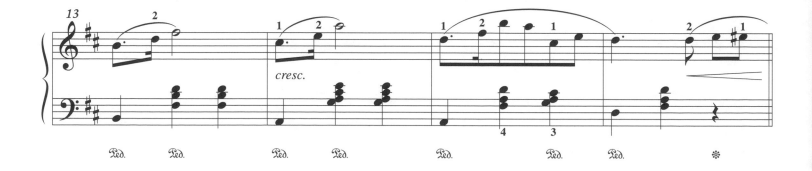

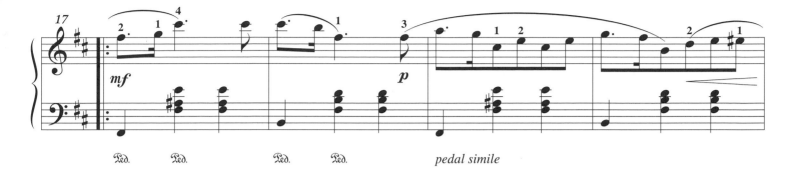

SOLDIERS' MARCH

(from *Album for the Young*)

ROBERT SCHUMANN
Op. 68, No. 2

Allegro

THE POOR ORPHAN

(from *Album for the Young*)

ROBERT SCHUMANN
Op. 68, No. 6

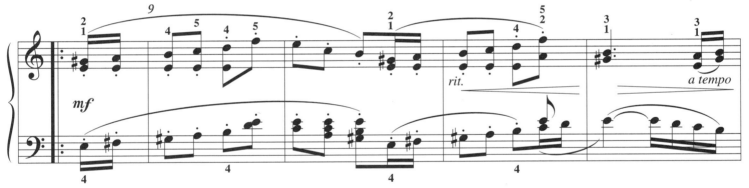

THE WILD HORSEMAN

(from *Album for the Young*)

ROBERT SCHUMANN
Op. 68, No. 8

Allegro con brio

KNECHT RUPRECHT

(from *Album for the Young*)

ROBERT SCHUMANN
Op. 68, No. 12

Allegro

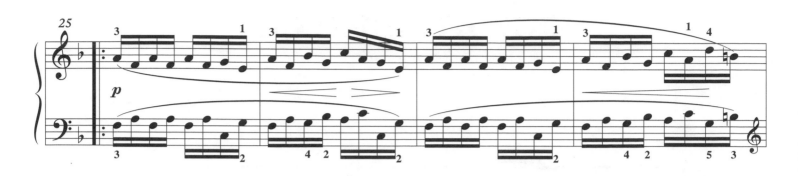

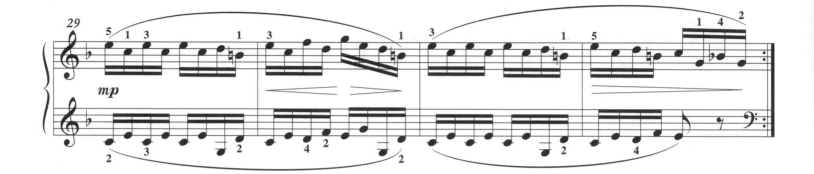

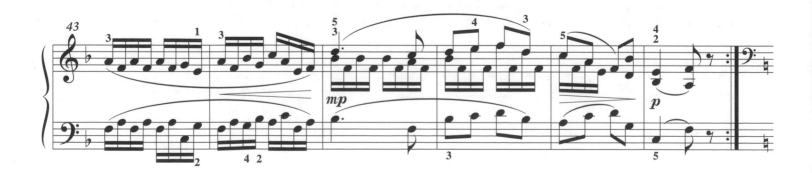

FIRST LOSS

(from *Album for the Young*)

ROBERT SCHUMANN
Op. 68, No. 16

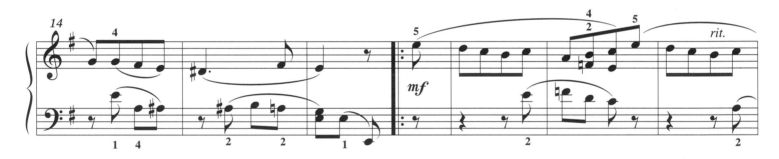

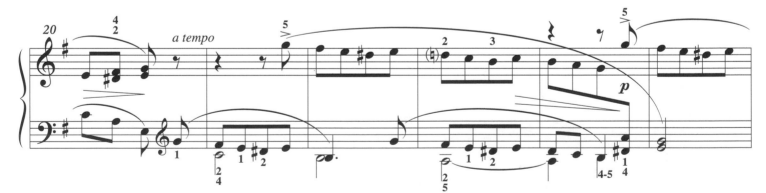

LITTLE ROMANCE

(from *Album for the Young*)

ROBERT SCHUMANN
Op. 68, No. 19

Non allegro

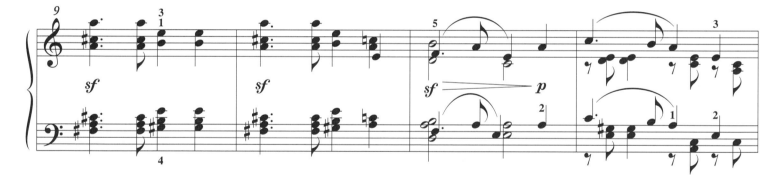

MORNING PRAYER

(from *Children's Album*)

PETER ILYICH TCHAIKOVSKY
Op. 39, No. 1

Tranquillo

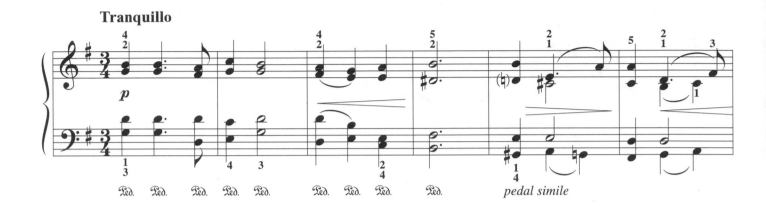

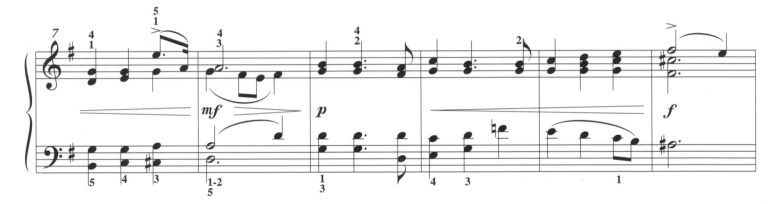

OLD FRENCH SONG

(from *Children's Album*)

PETER ILYICH TCHAIKOVSKY
Op. 39, No. 16

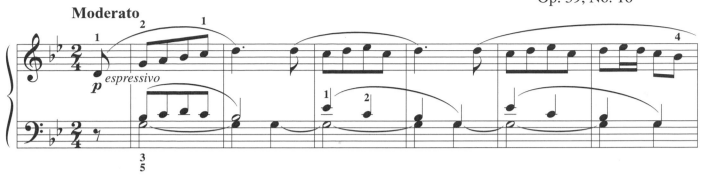

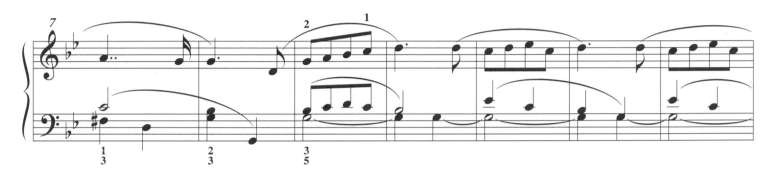

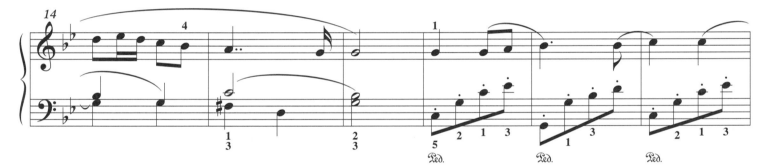

THE NEW DOLL

(from *Children's Album*)

PETER ILYICH TCHAIKOVSKY
Op. 39, No. 6

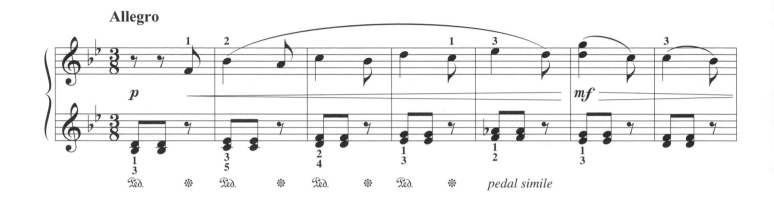

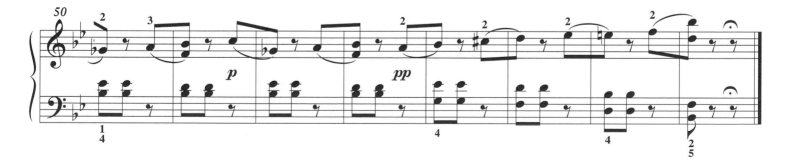

THE DOLL'S ILLNESS

(from *Children's Album*)

PETER ILYICH TCHAIKOVSKY
Op. 39, No. 7

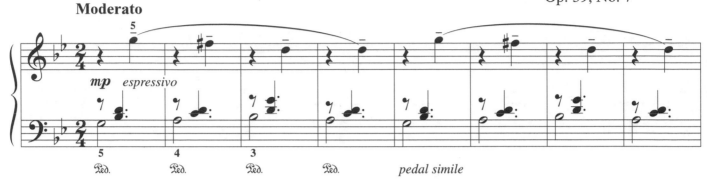

THE DOLL'S FUNERAL

(from *Children's Album*)

PETER ILYICH TCHAIKOVSKY
Op. 39, No. 8

Adagio

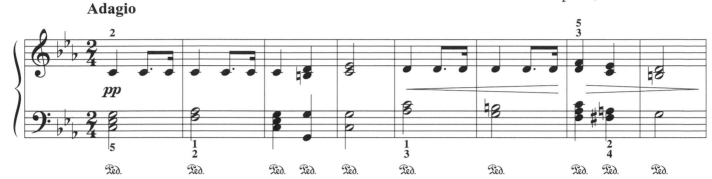

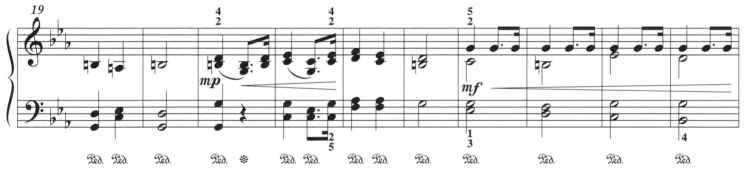

AT CHURCH

(from *Children's Album*)

PETER ILYICH TCHAIKOVSKY
Op. 39, No. 23

Moderato

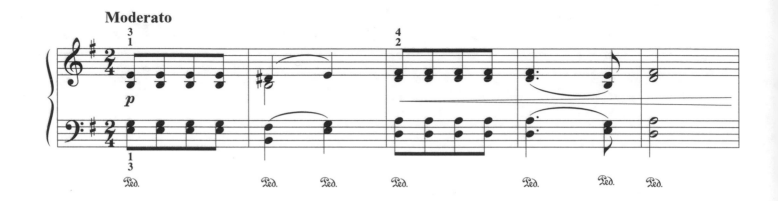

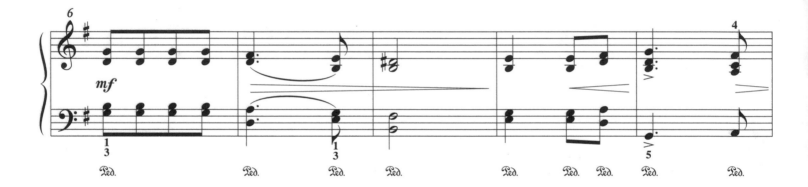

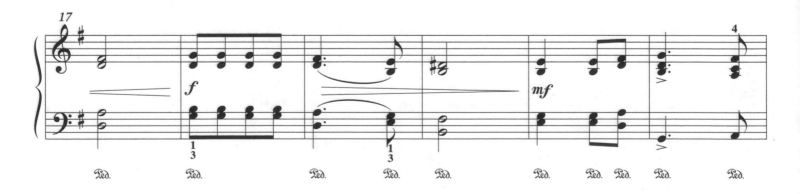

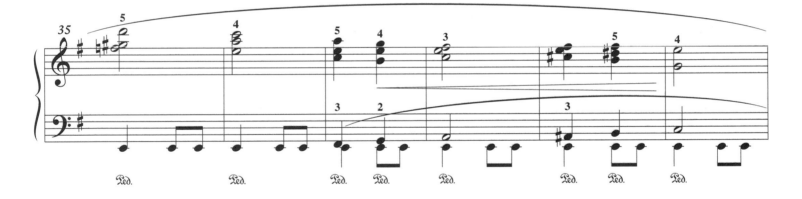

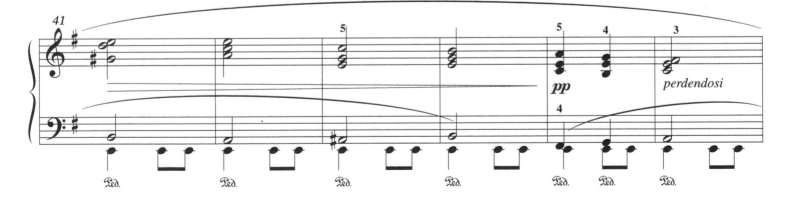

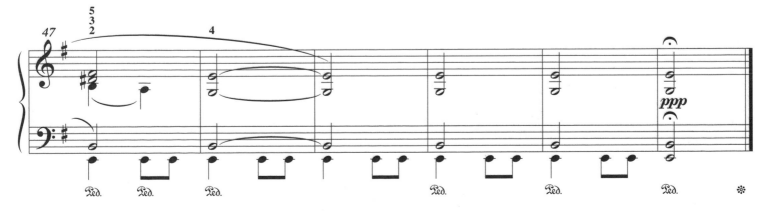

THE ORGAN-GRINDER SINGS

(from *Children's Album*)

PETER ILYICH TCHAIKOVSKY
Op. 39, No. 24

Tranquillo

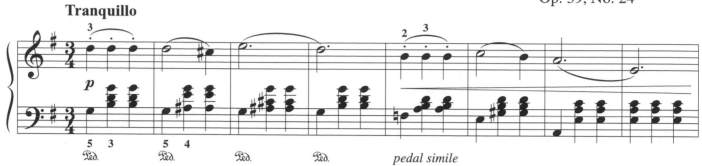

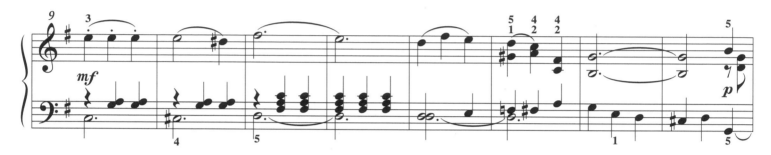

THE
TWENTIETH CENTURY

(1900 – 2000)

PEASANT SONG

(No. 1 from *Ten Easy Piano Pieces*)

BÉLA BARTÓK

Allegro moderato

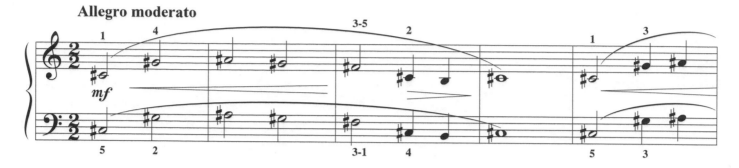

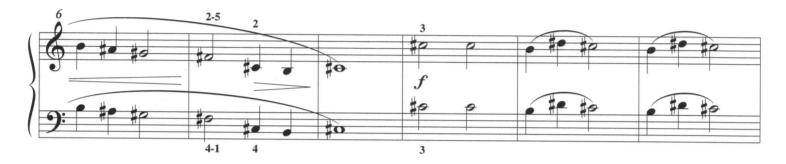

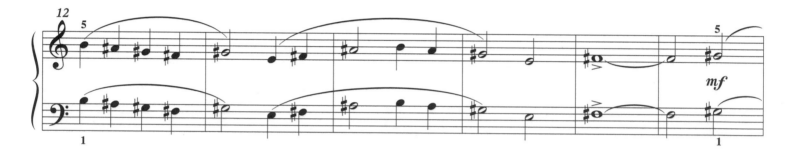

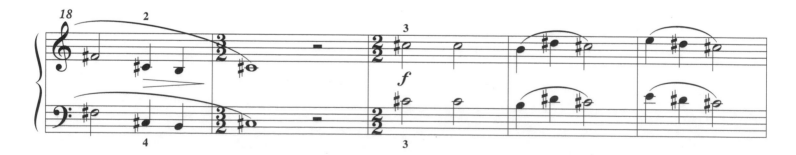

MINUET
(No. 11 from *First Term at the Piano*)

BÉLA BARTÓK

Andante grazioso

FF1392

HUNGARIAN FOLK SONG

(No. 13 from *First Term at the Piano*)

BÉLA BARTÓK

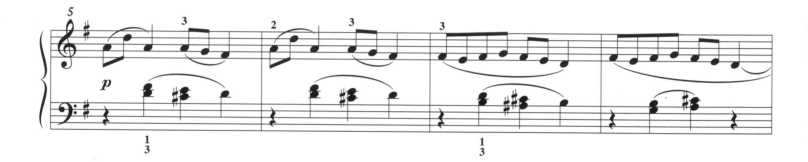

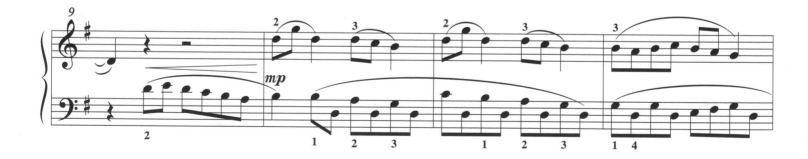

ANDANTE

(No. 14 from *First Term at the Piano*)

BÉLA BARTÓK

WALTZ

(No. 18 from *First Term at the Piano*)

BÉLA BARTÓK

Moderato

DOCTOR GRADUS AD PARNASSUM

(from *Children's Corner Suite*)

CLAUDE DEBUSSY

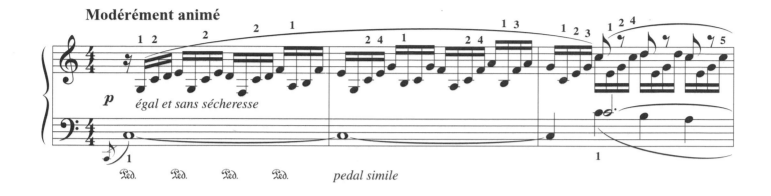

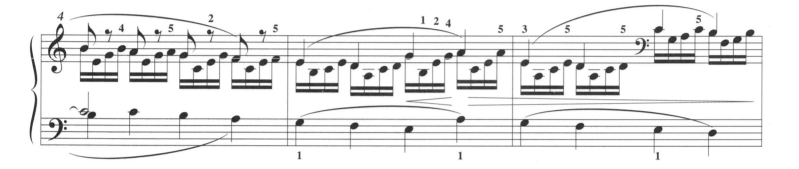

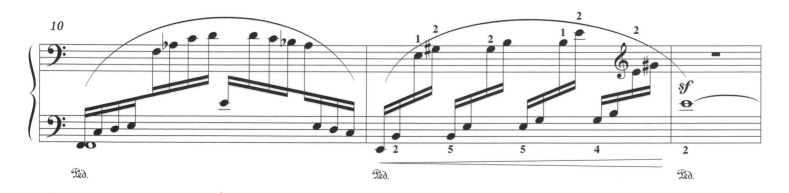

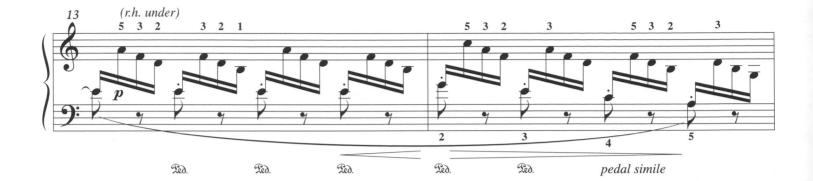

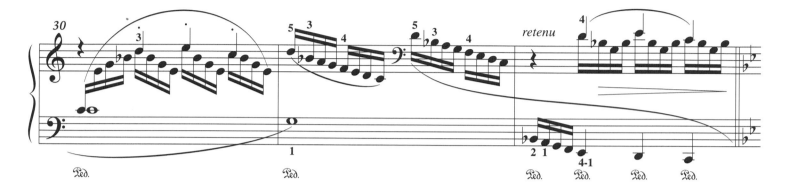

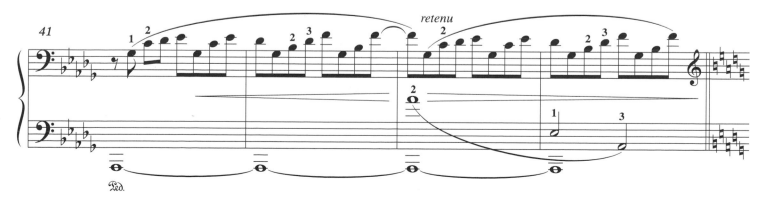

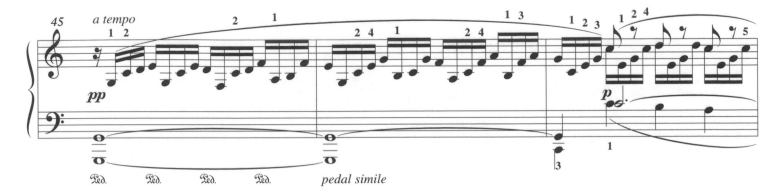

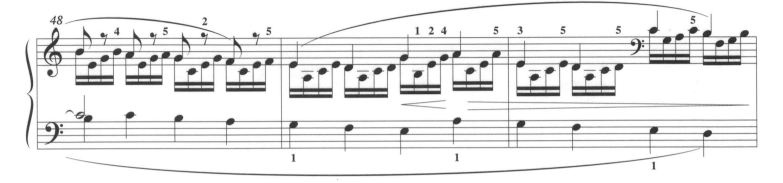

En animant peu á peu

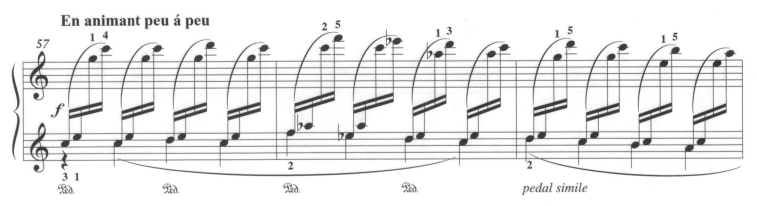

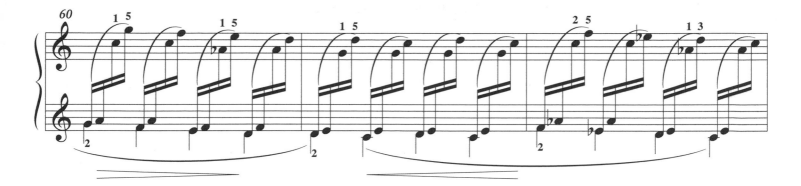

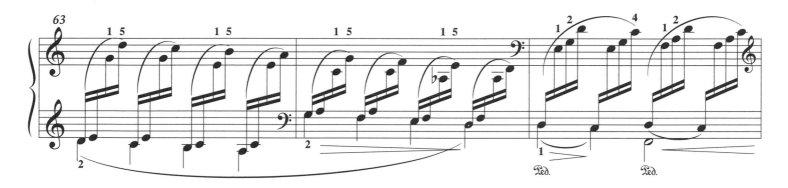

Très animé

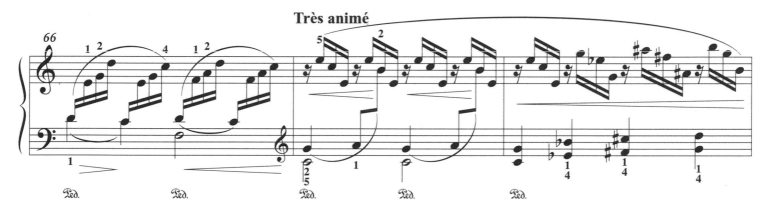

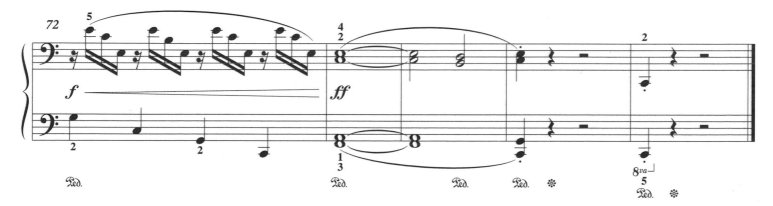

GYMNOPEDIE

(No. 3 from *Trois Gymnopedies*)

ERIK SATIE

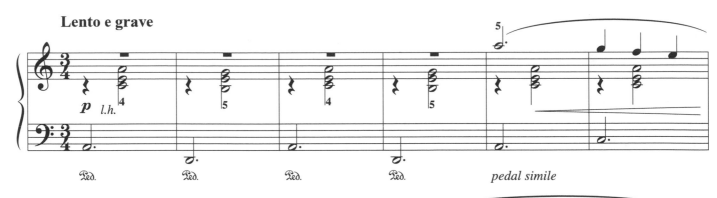

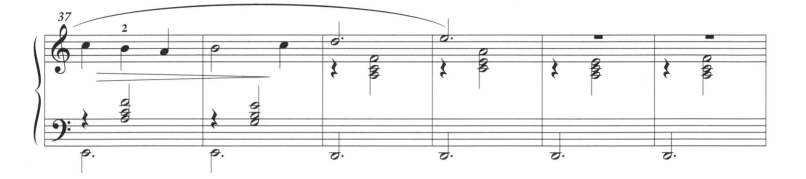

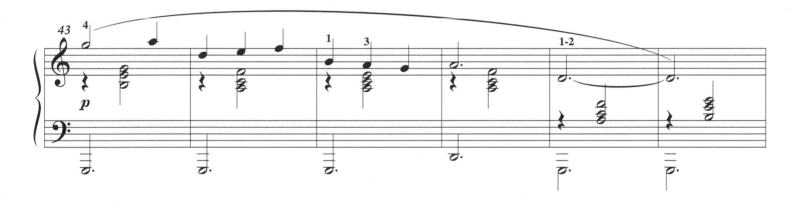

dedicated to James Brown and his Mandolin Club

THE ENTERTAINER

(A Rag Time Two Step)

SCOTT JOPLIN

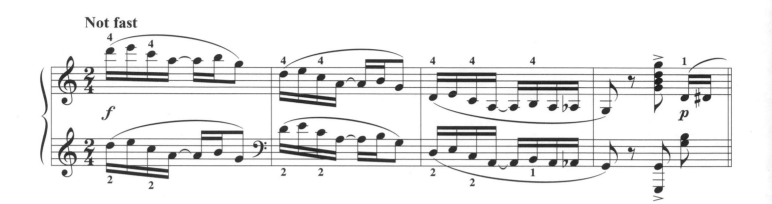

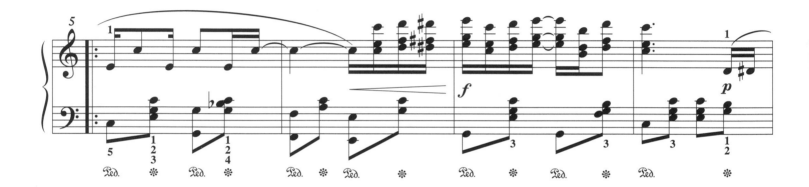

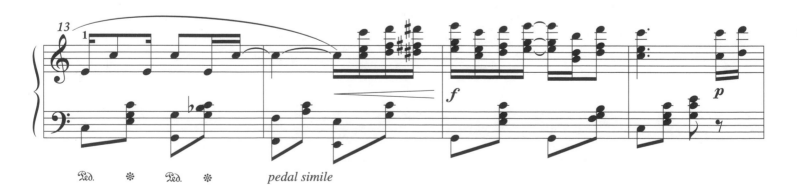

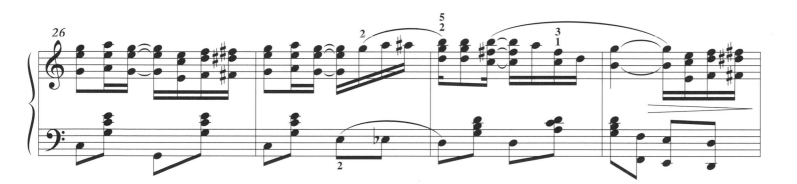

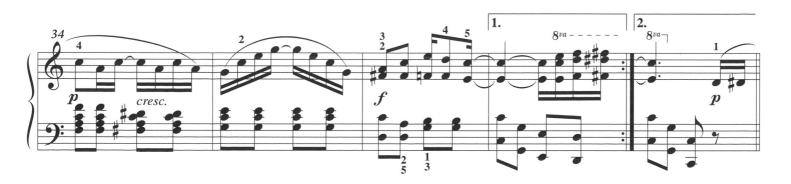

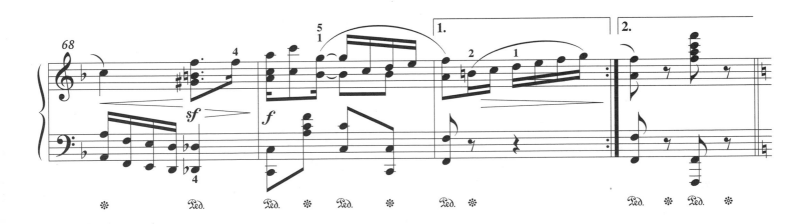

PIANO ARRANGEMENTS OF
ORCHESTRAL, VOCAL, & CHAMBER WORKS

CANON IN D

JOHANN PACHELBEL
Arranged by ROBERT SCHULTZ

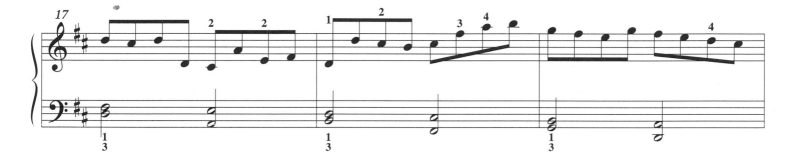

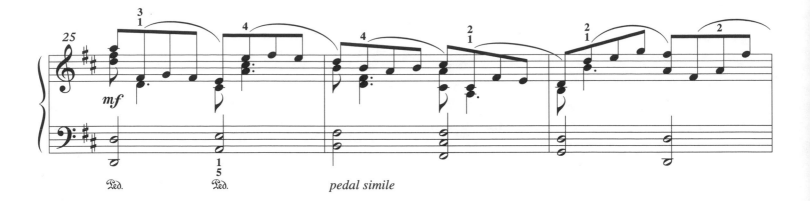

AVE MARIA

GIULIO CACCINI
Arranged by ROBERT SCHULTZ

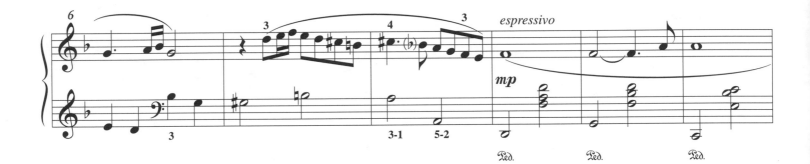

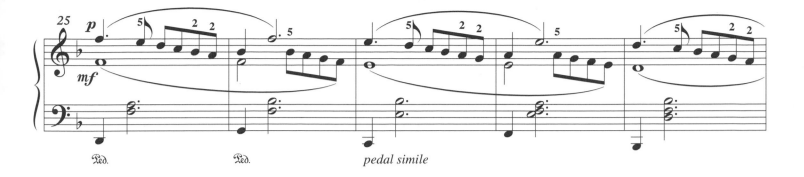

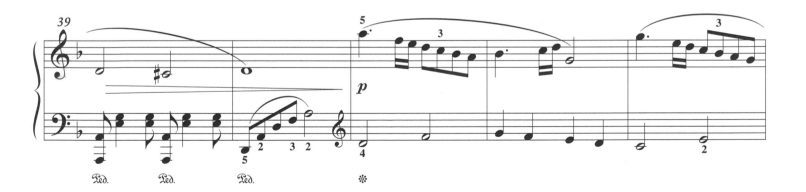

RONDEAU THEME

(from "Symphonic Suite No. 1")

JEAN JOSEPH MOURET
Arranged by ROBERT SCHULTZ

Allegro maestoso

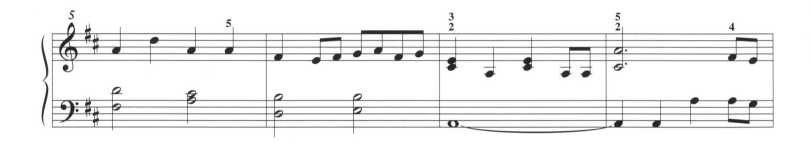

FUNERAL MARCH OF A MARIONETTE

CHARLES GOUNOD
Arranged by ROBERT SCHULTZ

Misterioso

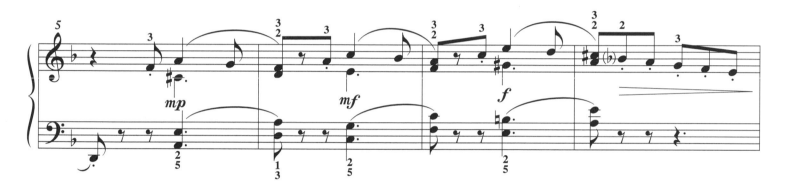

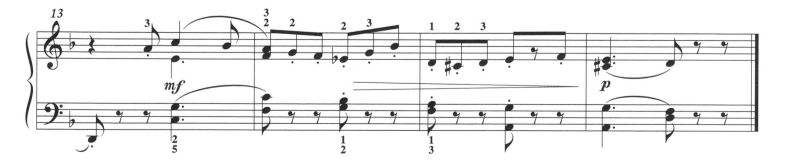

THE WEDDING MARCH

(from *A Midsummer Night's Dream*)

FELIX MENDELSSOHN
Arranged by ROBERT SCHULTZ

Maestoso

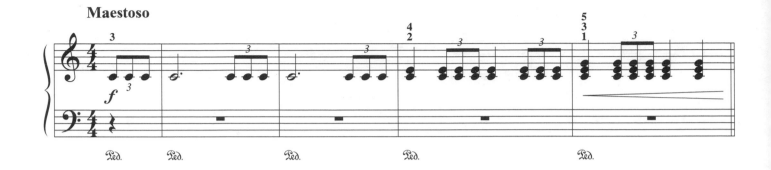

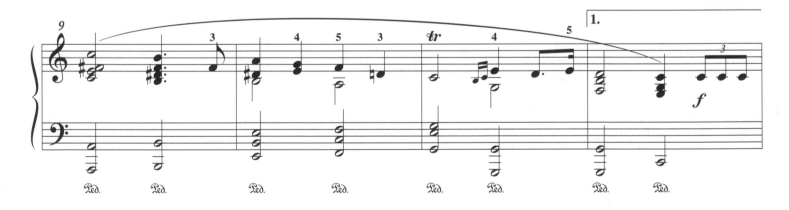

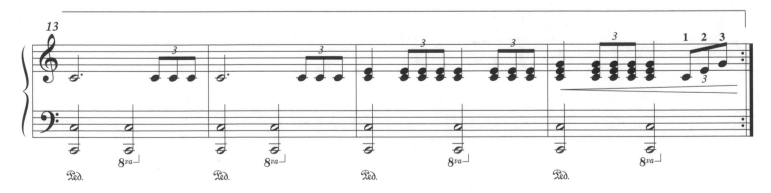

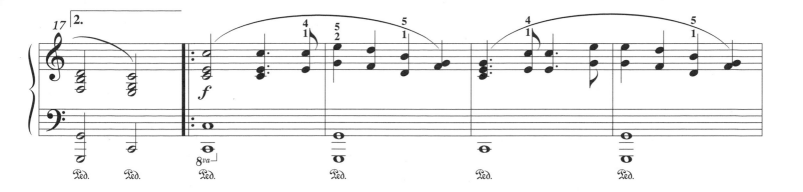

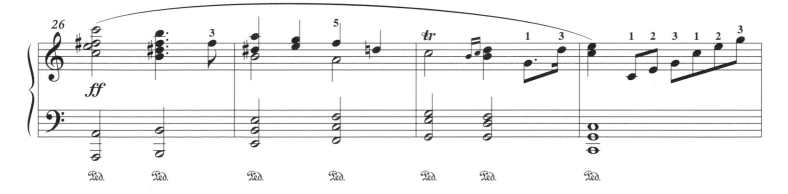

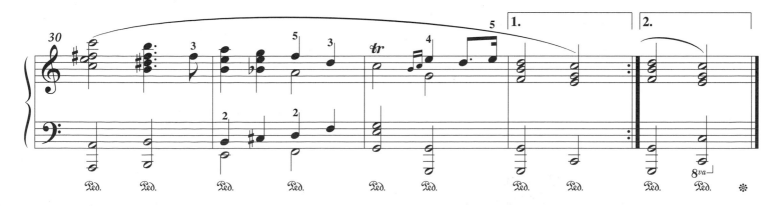

POMP AND CIRCUMSTANCE

EDWARD ELGAR
Arranged by ROBERT SCHULTZ

Largamente

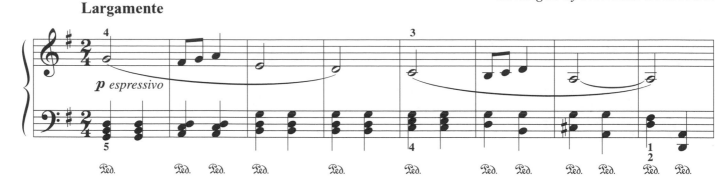

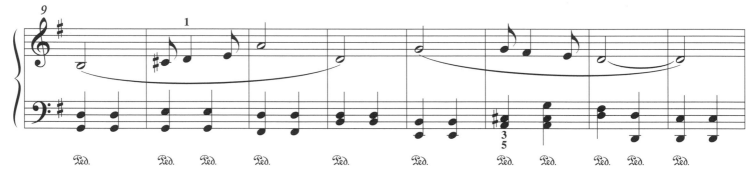

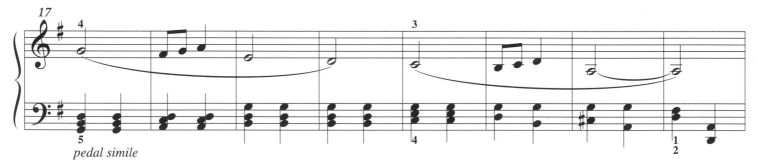

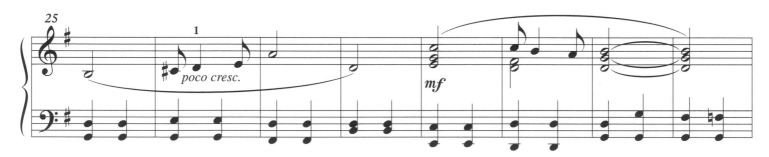

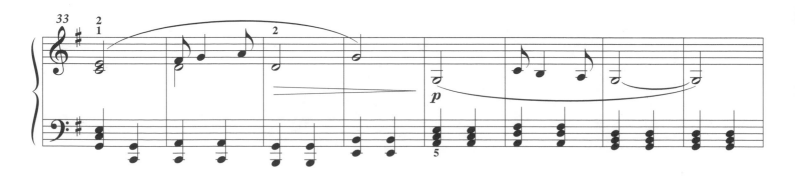

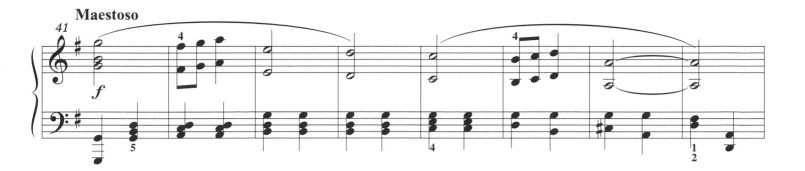

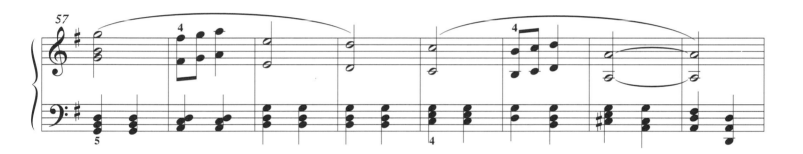

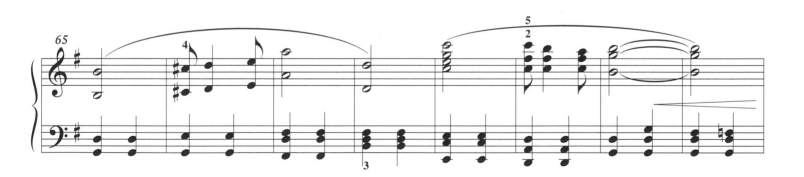

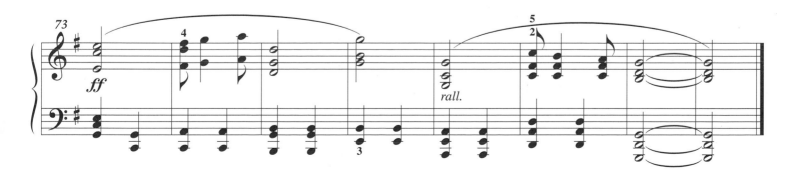

Theme from

SYMPHONY No. 1

(Movement IV)

JOHANNES BRAHMS
Arranged by ROBERT SCHULTZ

Theme from
SYMPHONY No. 3
(Movement III)

JOHANNES BRAHMS
Arranged by ROBERT SCHULTZ

Poco Allegretto

Theme from

SYMPHONY No. 5

(Movement I)

PETER ILYICH TCHAIKOVSKY
Arranged by ROBERT SCHULTZ

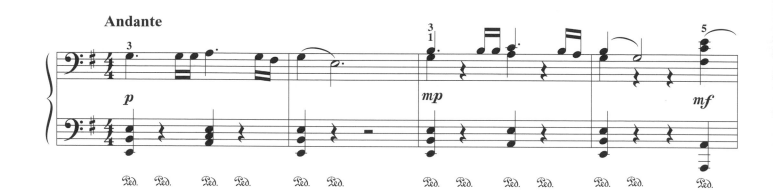

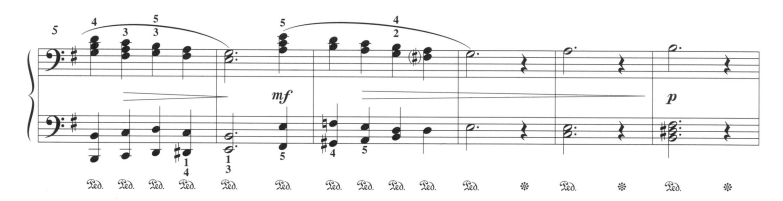

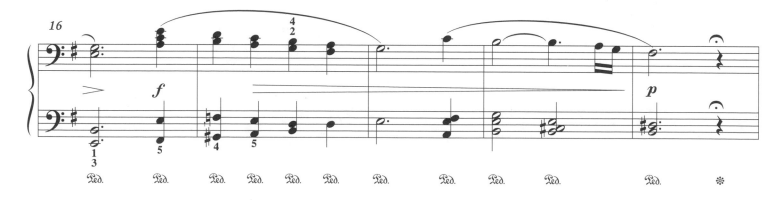

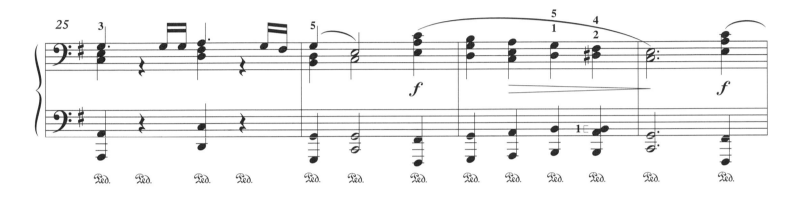

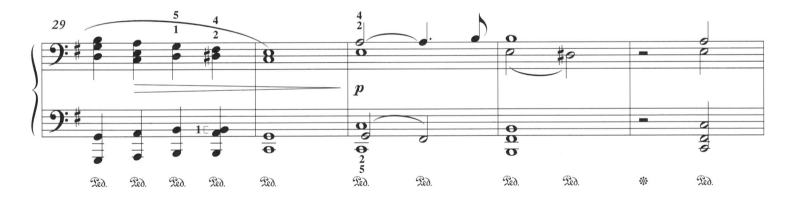

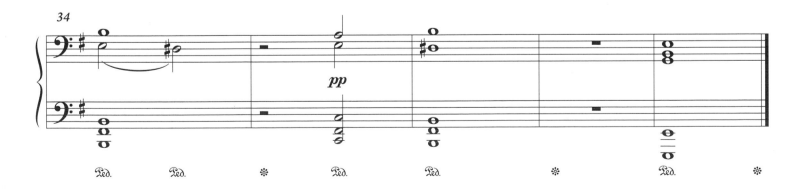

Theme from

THE NEW WORLD SYMPHONY

(Symphony No. 9, Movement II)

ANTONÍN DVOŘÁK
Arranged by ROBERT SCHULTZ

Largo
espressivo

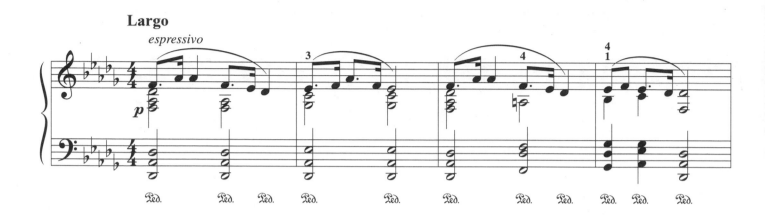

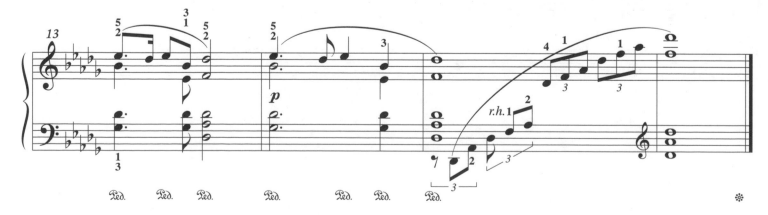

Table of Symbols

>	accent	*mf*	mezzo forte	*r.h., m.d.*	right hand
,	breath mark	*mp*	mezzo piano		rolled chord
⊕	coda		mordent	*sf*	sforzando
<	crescendo	8ᵛᵃ⌐	octave above		sign (segno)
>	diminuendo, decrescendo	8ᵛᵃ⌐	octave below		staccato
⌒	fermata	Ped.	pedal down		tenuto
f	forte	✳	pedal up	*t.c.*	tre corde
ff	fortissimo	*pp*	pianissimo	*tr*	trill
♪	grace note	*p*	piano	∾	turn
l.h., m.s., m.g.	left hand	‖: :‖	repeat	*u.c.*	una corda

Tempo Marks

Grave. Very slow, serious, solemn; the slowest tempo in music.

Largo. Broad, large; a degree faster than *grave.*

Larghetto. A degree faster than *largo.*

Lento. Slow.

Adagio. Slow, at ease; a degree faster than *lento.*

Andante. Walking, graceful.

Andantino. Moderately slow, flowing with ease; a degree faster than *andante.*

Moderato. Moderate.

Allegretto. Moderately quick, cheerful; a degree slower than *allegro.*

Allegro. Lively, quick, cheerful.

Vivace. Fast, brisk, vivacious.

Presto. Very fast, rapid.

Prestissimo. As fast as possible.

Glossary

Accelerando. abbr. *accel.* Accelerating, gradually becoming faster.

Accent. Denotes a special stress or emphasis upon a certain note or group of notes. In piano music, the two accent symbols most often encountered are > and − . > indicates a strong accent, and − *(tenuto)* indicates a slight stress or pressure and that the note should be held for its full value. Also see *sforzando.*

Ad libitum. At liberty. An indication that gives the performer liberty to alter the tempo of a passage, typically becoming somewhat slower and less strict than the established tempo.

Alla breve. (¢) A tempo mark indicating that the primary beat is given to the half note, $\frac{2}{2}$ rather than $\frac{4}{4}$.

Animé. Animated.

Animato. Animated, lively.

Assai. Much.

A tempo. In time. A direction to return to a previously established tempo after a brief departure from that tempo.

Breath mark. (ᦏ) In vocal, brass, or wind music, indicates points where it is recommended that the player take a breath. In piano or other types of music, the symbol indicates a slight pause, as if taking a breath in a vocal style.

Brio. Vigor, spirit.

Cantabile. In a singing style.

Coda. Tail. (⊕) A relatively brief section of music that occurs at the end of a piece or movement, providing a definitive closing. ⊕ is commonly used to indicate the point where the coda begins.

Con. With.

Crescendo. abbr. *cresc.* Specifies an increasing volume of sound; gradually becoming louder; also indicated by the symbol ◁ .

Da capo. abbr. *D.C.* From the beginning. Instruction to play again (repeat) from the beginning. *D.C. al Fine* indicates to play again from the beginning to the place marked *Fine* (end). *D.C. al Coda* indicates to play again from the beginning until arriving at the instruction to proceed directly to the coda (*To Coda* ⊕).

Dal segno. abbr. *D.S.* From the sign. Instruction to play again (repeat) from the sign (𝄋). *D.S. al Fine* indicates to play again from the sign (𝄋) to the place marked *Fine* (end). *D.S. al Coda* indicates to play again from the sign (𝄋) until arriving at the instruction to proceed directly to the coda (*To Coda* ⊕).

Diminuendo. abbr. *dim.* Specifies a decreasing volume of sound; gradually becoming softer; also indicated by the word *decrescendo (decresc.)* and the symbol ▷ .

Dolce. Sweet, delicate.

Égal. Even.

Espressivo. abbr. *espr.* Expressively. Commonly used to denote a melodic phrase or passage to be projected (stand out) and performed with great expression.

Fermata. A pause or hold represented by the sign ⌢ . The note(s) marked by this sign are to be sustained for a longer-than-normal duration.

Fine. End.

Forte. abbr. *f*. Loud, strong.

Fortissimo. abbr. *ff*. Very loud, very strong.

Fortississimo. abbr. *fff*. As loud as possible.

Giocoso. Humorous.

Grace note. (♪) An ornamental note used to embellish a melodic tone. Grace notes are normally printed in smaller type, immediately preceding the note that they embellish, and are not counted in the rhythm of the measure.

Grazioso. Graceful.

Largamente. Broadly.

Left hand. abbr. *l.h.* Indicates a note or passage to be played by the left hand. In Italian, *mano sinistra (m.s.)*; in French, *main gauche (m.g.).*

Legato. Bound, slurred. A direction to perform the marked passage in a smooth and connected manner, without interruption between the tones; also indicated by a curved line over or under the passage.

Leggiero. Light, nimble.

Maestoso. Majestic.

Marcato. Marked, accented, to be played with distinct emphasis and precision.

Meno. Less.

Mezzo forte. abbr. *mf*. Half loud, moderately loud.

Mezzo piano. abbr. *mp*. Half soft, moderately soft.

Misterioso. Mysterious.

Molto. Much, very. *Molto rit.,* becoming much slower; *molto allegro,* very fast.

Mosso. Moved, movement, motion. *Meno mosso,* less movement, slower; *più mosso,* more movement, faster.

Moto. Motion.

Non. Not, no.

Octave marks. When positioned above a note or group of notes, the symbol $8^{va}\lceil$ indicates that the note(s) are to be played one octave higher than written. When positioned beneath a note or group of notes, the symbol $8^{va}\rfloor$ indicates that the note(s) are to be played one octave lower than written.

Pedal. A mechanism or part of an instrument that is manipulated by the foot. See also *sostenuto* and *una corda.* As applied to the piano, the term is commonly used to refer to the right pedal, or damper pedal, which when depressed raises all of the dampers allowing any or all strings to vibrate freely. The abbreviation *Ped.* is shown in piano music at specific points where the damper pedal is to be depressed. The appearance of a subsequent *Ped.* indicates that the pedal is to be quickly released and redepressed, or "changed." The symbol ❋ is used to indicate specific points where the pedal is to be released. Another common system uses a solid line placed beneath the bass staff to indicate that the damper pedal is to be depressed (└───), changed (──∧──) or released (───┘).

Perdendosi. Dying away.

Peu á peu. Little by little.

Pianissimo. abbr. *pp*. Very soft.

Pianississimo. abbr. *ppp*. As soft as possible.

Piano. abbr. *p*. Soft.

Più. More.

Poco. Little, slight. *Poco rit.,* gradually becoming a little slower; *un poco,* a little.

Poco a poco. By degrees, little by little.

Rallentando. abbr. *rall.* Becoming gradually slower; same as *ritardando.*

Repeat. The signs ‖: at the beginning and :‖ at the end of a section specify that the section is to be repeated. If the latter sign appears alone, the repetition is to be taken from the beginning of the composition.

Retenu. Held back. *Un peu retenu,* a little held back.

Right hand. abbr. *r.h.* Indicates a note or passage to be played by the right hand. In Italian, *mano destra (m.d.)*; in French, *main droite (m.d.).*

Risoluto. Resolute, resolved.

Ritardando. abbr. *rit.* Becoming gradually slower; same as *rallentando. Ritenuto* indicates an immediate tempo reduction.

Rolled chord. In piano music, ⸘ placed to the left of a chord indicates that the notes of the chord are to be sounded from lowest to highest in a slightly broken manner.

Rubato. Robbed. Indicates a style of performance that incorporates a flexible approach to interpreting the duration of note values, allowing certain notes to be elongated and others quickened.

Sans. Without.

Scherzando. Playful.

Sec. Dry. *Sécheresse,* dryness.

Segno. Sign. (𝄋) See *Dal segno.*

Sempre. Always, continually, still.

Senza. Without. *Senza sordini,* without mutes (dampers), i.e., to be sustained.

Sforzando. abbr. *sf.* Forced. An indication to sound the note or notes marked with a sudden and striking emphasis; a powerful accent.

Simile. abbr. *sim.* Similarly. A direction to continue to perform a certain action (articulation, pedal, etc.) in the same manner as previously indicated.

Slentando. Relaxing the time, gradually slowing.

Smorzando. Dying away.

Sostenuto. 1. Sustained. 2. The middle pedal of the three commonly found on modern pianos. Its purpose is to sustain an isolated tone or group of tones without raising all of the dampers, which occurs when the damper pedal is depressed. The damper(s) that the player wishes to isolate must first be raised by depressing the corresponding key(s). Once raised, those dampers may be locked into this position by depressing the sostenuto pedal. Most spinet and upright pianos do not have a true sostenuto function. On these pianos, the middle pedal commonly serves as a damper pedal for the bass register only. The term *sostenuto,* or its abbreviation *sos.,* is shown at specific points where the sostenuto pedal is to be depressed. The symbol ✻ is shown at specific points where the sostenuto pedal is to be released. The two instructions will normally be connected by a broken line (*sos.*- - - -✻) to eliminate any confusion caused by damper pedal instructions that can occur simultaneously.

Sotto. Under. *Sotto voce* (under the voice), to be performed in an undertone, subdued.

Spiritoso. Spirited, witty.

Staccato. Detached, disconnected, shortened. Indicated by a small dot placed above or below a note.

Subito. abbr. *sub.* Suddenly. *Subito pp,* suddenly very soft.

Tempo. Time. The speed or degree of motion of a composition or section of a composition.

Tenuto. Held. Indicated by a short stroke placed above or below a note directing that it is to be sustained for its full value; also used to indicate a slight accent or stress.

Tranquillo. Tranquil, calm.

Tre corde. abbr. *t.c.* Three strings. Used in piano music to indicate the release of the left pedal (una corda pedal, or soft pedal).

Très. Very.

Trill. The rapid alternation of two adjacent notes.

Troppo. Too (much). *Allegro ma non troppo,* fast but not too much.

Una corda. abbr. *u.c.* One string. Used in piano music to direct that the left pedal (una corda pedal, sometimes called soft pedal) be depressed. The instruction *t.c.* (tre corde) directs that the pedal be released. On grand pianos, depressing this pedal causes the entire action mechanism and keyboard to shift slightly to the right so that the hammers will strike only one (or two) of the two (or three) strings assigned to each note, producing a more delicate, muted tone. On upright and spinet pianos, the una corda pedal will also create a muted effect by moving the hammers closer to the strings or by causing a strip of felt to rest lightly on the strings.

Voce. Voice.

Title Index

The Composers

The Baroque Period (1600 – 1750)
Carl Philipp Emanuel Bach . . . . .March 8, 1714 – December 15, 1788
Johann Sebastian Bach . . . . .March 21, 1685 – July 28, 1750
Giulio Caccini . . . . .c. 1545 – December, 1618
Arcangelo Corelli . . . . .February 17, 1653 – January 8, 1713
George Frideric Handel . . . . .February 23, 1685 – April 14, 1759
Jean Joseph Mouret . . . . .April 16, 1682 – December 22, 1738
Johann Pachelbel . . . . .August ?, 1653 – March 6/7, 1706
Domenico Scarlatti . . . . .October 26, 1685 – July 23, 1757
Georg Philipp Telemann . . . . .March 14, 1681 – June 25, 1767

The Classical Period (1750 – 1820)
Ludwig van Beethoven . . . . .December 15/16, 1770 – March 26, 1827
Muzio Clementi . . . . .January 23, 1752 – March 10, 1832
Franz Joseph Haydn . . . . .March 31, 1732 – May 31, 1809
Friedrich Kuhlau . . . . .September 11, 1786 – March 12, 1832
Leopold Mozart . . . . .November 14, 1719 – May 28, 1787
Wolfgang Amadeus Mozart . . . . .January 27, 1756 – December 5, 1791
Daniel Gottlob Türk . . . . .August 10, 1750 – August 26, 1813

The Romantic Period (1820 – 1900)
Johannes Brahms . . . . .May 7, 1833 – April 3, 1897
Johann Friedrich Burgmüller . . . . .December 4, 1806 – February 13, 1874
Frédéric Chopin . . . . .March 1, 1810 – October 17, 1849
Antonín Dvořák . . . . .September 8, 1841 – May 1, 1904
Edward Elgar . . . . .June 2, 1857 – February 23, 1934
Charles Gounod . . . . .June 18, 1818 – October 18, 1893
Edward MacDowell . . . . .December 18, 1860 – January 23, 1908
Felix Mendelssohn . . . . .February 3, 1809 – November 4, 1847
Franz Schubert . . . . .January 31, 1797 – November 19, 1828
Robert Schumann . . . . .June 8, 1810 – July 29, 1856
Peter Ilyich Tchaikovsky . . . . .May 7, 1840 – November 6, 1893

The Twentieth Century (1900 – 2000)
Béla Bartók . . . . .March 25, 1881 – September 26, 1945
Claude Debussy . . . . .August 22, 1862 – March 25, 1918
Scott Joplin . . . . .1868 – 1917
Erik Satie . . . . .May 17, 1866 – July 1, 1925